Teaching Secondary Mathematics as if the Planet Matters

Teaching Secondary Mathematics as if the Planet Matters explores how mathematics teachers can develop approaches to curriculum and learning that help students understand the nature of the contemporary world. It sets out a model for teaching and learning that allows teachers to examine existing approaches to teaching and draw upon the insights of mathematics as a discipline to help students relate classroom mathematics to global issues such as climate change, the economy, food supplies, biodiversity, human rights and social justice.

Including practical examples, suggestions for teaching activities and detailed further reading sections, this book covers:

- the mathematics of description in the measuring, recording and statistical analysis that informs our knowledge of climate change, consumption and sustainability;
- the mathematics of prediction in the modelling used by governments, scientists and businesses to plan roads, power stations and food supplies and their effects;
- the mathematics of communication in the news reports, blogs and environmental campaigns, incomplete without graphs, charts and statistics.

The true worth of a school subject is revealed in how far it can account for and respond to the major issues of the time. The issue of the environment cuts across subject boundaries and requires an interdisciplinary response. Mathematics teachers are part of that response and they have a crucial role in helping students to respond to environmental issues and representations.

Alf Coles is Senior Lecturer in Education at the University of Bristol, UK.

Richard Barwell is Professor of Education at the University of Ottawa, Canada.

Tony Cotton, now retired, was Associate Dean of the Carnegie Faculty of Sport and Education at Leeds Metropolitan University, UK.

Jan Winter, now retired, was Senior Lecturer in Mathematics Education at the University of Bristol, UK.

Laurinda Brown is Senior Lecturer in Mathematics Education at the University of Bristol, UK.

Teaching School Subjects as if the Planet Matters

Series Editors: John Morgan (University of Bristol and Institute of Education, London) and Sasha Matthewman (University of Bristol)

We live in a time when there are serious questions about the ability of the planet to sustain current levels of economic development. Future generations are likely to face a bleaker environmental future and will need to learn how to mitigate and adapt to the effects of climate change. However, despite the obvious importance of these issues, most schooling continues with little direct engagement with questions of environmental change.

The true worth of a school subject is revealed in how far it can account for and respond to the major issues of the time. This series aims to inform teachers about environmental issues and offer inspiration for teaching lessons with critical environmental awareness. It asserts that only by helping pupils to recognise and understand the multi-dimensional nature of these issues will they be able to contribute to society's attempts to deal with rapid natural and human-induced environmental change.

Teaching Secondary Mathematics as if the Planet Matters

Alf Coles, Richard Barwell,
Tony Cotton, Jan Winter and
Laurinda Brown

Routledge
Taylor & Francis Group

LONDON AND NEW YORK

First published 2013
by Routledge
2 Park Square, Milton Park, Abingdon, Oxon OX14 4RN

Simultaneously published in the USA and Canada
by Routledge
711 Third Avenue, New York, NY 10017

Routledge is an imprint of the Taylor & Francis Group, an informa business

British Library Cataloguing in Publication Data
A catalogue record for this book is available from the British Library

Library of Congress Cataloging in Publication Data
Teaching secondary mathematics as if the planet matters / Alf Coles,
Richard Barwell, Tony Cotton, Jan Winter and Laurinda Brown.
    pages cm
    1. Mathematics – Study and teaching (Secondary) 2. Environmental
education. I. Coles, Alf. II. Barwell, Richard, 1969– III. Cotton,
Tony. IV. Winter, Jan. V. Brown, Laurinda.
    QA11.2.T44 2013
    510.71´2–dc23   2012038625

ISBN: 978-0-415-68843-7 (hbk)
ISBN: 978-0-415-68844-4 (pbk)
ISBN: 978-0-203-35728-6 (ebk)

Typeset in Bembo
by HWA Text and Data Management, London

MIX
Paper from
responsible sources
FSC   FSC® C013056
www.fsc.org

Printed and bound in Great Britain by
TJ International Ltd, Padstow, Cornwall

Contents

Figures

Tables

Preface

We would not have written this book without feeling, passionately at times, that there are global issues that threaten human life and which urgently need to be addressed in classrooms. However, throughout the book, we take a critical stance towards our own opinions and those of other authors. We aim to raise issues and questions and support readers in exploring these through mathematics-related activity without predetermining what any consequent actions could be. There are other books in this series that can be read to broaden perspectives on issues of sustainability, notably *Teaching Secondary Geography as if the Planet Matters* (Morgan 2011).

This book is arranged into two parts, with the first chapter of each part setting up themes. Part I looks at a range of global issues or challenges facing the planet. We have not attempted, in any way, to be exhaustive in the list of issues we have chosen. Instead, we offer examples of mathematical explorations of these issues. We have, in general, limited our explorations to mathematics that would be on a pre-16 syllabus. These chapters are not intended for direct classroom use, but do include some ideas for activities in school.

Part II is more directly classroom focused and begins from different curriculum headings. We offer activities in each chapter, with detail about a starting point and then pointers about possible ways the activity could go. These activities are generally aimed at the 11–16 age range, although most could be adapted for younger or older students.

We imagine teachers interested in particular issues using chapters from the first section. Teachers who have particular content to teach and who want ideas for contexts that will allow an exploration of wider issues can use chapters from Part II. However, in both sections we refer back to ideas raised in the first chapters of the section (Chapter 1 and Chapter 7) and we recommend you read these first.

The ideas and issues raised in this book are moving on rapidly and we have tried to reference web sites throughout the text that are likely to stay up to date and be renewed regularly.

So, how did we, five mathematics educators, come to be interested in writing this book? Here are our stories, which perhaps give a context to the chapters for which we are responsible. The decision to add names to chapters came late in the writing of this book and the early work of structuring the writing and sharing ideas for chapters was done collaboratively.

Alf

I remember as a teenager getting a book, *5000 Days to Save the Planet* (1990), which engrossed and scared me. Between school and university I spent a year teaching in Zimbabwe and, not surprisingly perhaps, became interested in issues around development and aid. At university, I worked for a charity raising money for Eritrean refugees in the Sudan, and went to Sudan one summer. As my degree was coming to a close, I applied for a Masters in Development Studies at the School of Oriental and African Studies (SOAS), in London, perhaps an equivalent fork in the road to Richard's VSO job, except in my case I wasn't offered a place on the course. So, I then applied to the Eritrean consulate to go out to Eritrea as a teacher – imagining I might go for a couple of years. As I was there I saw another side of 'aid' and 'development', for example a shipment of fur lined boots arriving at the school (from Sweden I think, the temperature in Eritrea was rarely cold), there was a barn full of donated, unused equipment (e.g., microfiche) and one that trumped most was that the school was supplied with powdered milk from the EU (it was in a remote area of Eritrea, the diet was limited, with few opportunities to get minerals and vitamins) and one day the shipment came through and it was all powdered skimmed milk ... I also reflected on what impact my own role was having and it pains me still to think of one boy from a local nomadic family who got quite friendly with me and another British teacher in the school, and then we left and what had we done really except shown him an image of unattainable wealth. Part way through the year in Eritrea, as I was wondering what to do next, I realised I was actually loving the teaching (which had not been the reason for going). PGCE and teaching jobs followed. I do periodically think, how bad will crises have to become to provoke me to leave my day job and campaign; however, as with Richard, I am not sure how good an activist I would be ...

Richard

I was interested in environmental issues at school. I grew up in a largely rural area, close to a canal, woodland, farmland and so on. I spent much of my adolescence mucking around in streams, walking the fields or cycling round the countryside. Later, I joined Greenpeace and Friends of the Earth and other organisations and read their publications – climate change was already a concern in those circles. At university, I was a member of the Green Society. As a teacher, I volunteered with the British Trust for Conservation Volunteers, leading or participating in working holidays in some beautiful parts of the UK, including the Yorkshire Dales, the Lake District, the Western Isles and the Shetland Isles. These activities heightened my awareness of environmental issues (and bird watching). Indeed, when I left my teaching position in Yorkshire, I had *two* options lined up. I signed up with Voluntary Service Overseas (VSO), but the alternative was a place offered on a postgraduate course in conservation management. VSO came off and I went to Pakistan, otherwise I would now be a park ranger. Climate change has become a real concern and I decided that I should do something about it. Where I lived in Pakistan is dependent on water from glaciers. The options were to give up my job and become an activist (I'm not sure I'd be a very good one) or to use my work to provoke more thinking about it.

Tony

I have never had such a direct connection with 'sustainability' as a distinct set of issues. However, my political activism has always taken on an international dimension and impacted on the way I operate as a teacher. Freire said, 'I work, and working I transform the world' (1970: 15). I have always taken this to mean that the way we make a difference at an international level is to make a difference within the 'worlds' in which we operate. So, when I was a class teacher in the 1980s we would look at data from Nicaragua exploring the post-revolution developments in education and health, or the safety records of nuclear power plants. When I worked as an advisory teacher for multicultural education in the 1990s, we would explore the kinds of issues around 'development' that Alf mentions and problematise the images that many teachers and children had of the 'homelands' of many of their classmates.

I think that underpinning all of this are ideas of social justice and democracy. I believe that there are sufficient resources for us all to share and that the 'unfairness' which leads to famine and war will only be resolved through the development of democracy(s) based on ideas of social justice. So, I think there are political solutions to the issues of sustainability – and that the mathematics classroom is a place in which we can carry out political debate and so support our learners in becoming both informed about the way their world is and empowered to become critical thinkers in order to change the world(s) in which they exist.

Jan

My internationalist interests came initially from my siblings' travels, rather than my own. My sister spent most of her adult life in Asia in international development, with all its imperfections. I was always aware of the tensions, but somehow it seemed better than doing nothing. Similarly my brother worked for both VSO and the Intermediate Technology Development Group (ITDG) in Africa. I was left with a fascination for how different life could be from the basic capitalist model and I still struggle to understand the breadth of ways in which different people find pleasure in their lives – some of which seem to me to be impossibly hard. Sustainability is key to this as we try to find ways to support more people than seems feasible. I also struggle with my carbon footprint and my trip to India (November 2012) has plenty of guilt attached.

Another strand for me is my relationship with food, which led me to want to write Chapter 4. I became vegetarian (alright, a fish eater) following a trip to Canada in the early 1980s when the amount of meat being eaten by everyone on a regular basis seemed obscene. My rationale was about sustainable and humane farming, which is why I continued to eat fish. That position seems to be far less defensible now. Since then, I have moved into growing a lot of my own vegetables and feel that the connection with food that this gives me helps me understand ways of life that depend on good soil, climate and a vast amount of physical effort.

How all of this links with my teaching is less clear to me, but I think it simply comes down to my feeling that mathematical skills are fundamental to understanding and acting on the way the world is now, so that my contribution is in helping others gain those skills.

Laurinda

When I was in the sixth form at school, I joined the Council for Education in World Citizenship (CEWC) and attended a conference in London that is probably the nearest I have got to being an activist. As my chapter on the economy reveals, I have also been an avid reader of science fiction since I was 14. These two formative aspects of me are not contradictory because the science fiction that I prefer takes current issues and fast forwards to look at possible futures, in some cases powerfully imaging disaster scenarios and, at other times, exploring potential solutions. CEWC was an active group that explored world citizenship as a vehicle, say, for sharing food production and letting go of 'have' and 'have not' nations. We explored the feasibility of possible solutions.

I have a passion for woodland and am part of the Woodland Trust although as with Alf and Richard, my passions have been taken by teaching and challenging ideas, using the trading game (see Chapter 2), for instance, way back in 1993. What I have actually seen over my life in teaching has been a gradual splintering of national groupings, driven by politics rather than ethnicity (will Scotland be the next to cede, I wonder in December 2012?). When I'm low, it feels like we travel further and further away from world citizenship – however, if the politically motivated groupings fall away, maybe as individual citizens and family groupings we will learn to share at a sustainable local level? I do worry about my carbon footprint!

We would like to acknowledge the work of the series editors in making suggestions during the development of this book. John Morgan's *Teaching Secondary Geography as if the Planet Matters* (2011) has already been mentioned as a source of perspectives on sustainability and Sasha Matthewman's *Teaching Secondary English as if the Planet Matters* (2010) is another reference work to look at, for example to support the role of literature in envisioning alternative futures.

We would also like to thank those experts who read and commented on drafts of chapters or who engaged with us in conversations about the ideas in the book. In particular, Richard Barwell thanks Professor Brad deYoung, Memorial University, Newfoundland, Canada; Alf Coles thanks Peter Clegg, Fielden Clegg Bradley

Studios; Laurinda Brown thanks Carly Sawatzki, University of Monash, Australia. Any remaining errors are ours of course. Intelligent readers such as a medical doctor, Louise Younie, gave us the belief that there was a potential readership for this book from professionals who, with some support within the mathematics, can engage more deeply with the issues. Louise's comment was that she wished mathematics had been presented like this at school. We hope that you find that the planet matters through engaging with the activities and ideas that teach mathematics in this book.

References

Goldsmith, E. (1990) *5000 Days to Save the Planet*. London: Hamlyn.

Matthewman, S. (2010) *Teaching Secondary English as if the Planet Matters*. London: Routledge.

Morgan, J. (2011) *Teaching Secondary Geography as if the Planet Matters*. London: Routledge.

Freire, P. (1966) *Pedagogy of the Oppressed*. London: Penguin.

Part I
A critical stance on global issues

The role of mathematics in shaping our world

Richard Barwell

There are seven billion human beings on the planet Earth. This fact is simultaneously about sustainability and mathematics. First, sustainability: how can our planet support seven billion people? How much do seven billion people consume? What effect does this consumption have on the planet, on its forests, deserts, oceans and air? What will happen when the population reaches eight or nine or ten billion? What will happen if consumption continues to increase? These are primarily questions of sustainability: they are questions about the changing nature of the planetary ecosystem. A planet with seven billion people seems to be different from a planet with many fewer people. If you are reading this book, you may think some of these differences, including pollution, species loss and climate change, are cause for concern.

Now, mathematics: how many is seven billion? Can you visualise seven billion people? Or seven billion anythings? Where does this figure come from? How is it calculated? How is the population of the planet changing? How many people can the Earth sustain? How much do seven billion people consume? Think about seven billion breakfasts or toothbrushes or pairs of shoes. To make sense of a statement as innocuous as 'there are seven billion human beings on the planet Earth' involves a good deal of mathematics and of mathematical literacy.

These questions illustrate how sustainability and mathematics are inseparably linked. Of course, sustainability is about much more than global population: it is about finding a way for us all to 'tread lightly' on the Earth; a way for us to live without, perhaps, destroying much of the ecosystem that supports us. Much of what we know about the Earth and the changes that are happening to it is, however, based on mathematics, including counting, measuring, estimating and modelling. While mathematics is not the only way to learn about the Earth, it is an important and widespread one. Mathematics certainly provides a powerful way to understand the Earth on a planetary scale, beyond the range of individual perception. Mathematics, however, is more than simply a way to understand the world: It also shapes our world, particularly through technology. We have written this book because we want our students to learn mathematics so that they may better understand our Earth, our technological society and the impact of those seven billion people. We argue that mathematics teachers can address issues of sustainability in their teaching and we suggest some ways in which this could be achieved. This book, then, is about teaching mathematics as if the planet matters.

The purpose of this chapter is to introduce some general concepts that inform the rest of the book. These concepts are based on an approach called critical mathematics education. They are about the role that mathematics plays in modern society, how this role relates to sustainability and the way mathematics teaching can prepare students to be active citizens, able to both use and critique mathematics for a more sustainable future. To begin, however, I look first at what we mean by sustainability, and then at how mathematics is used to understand different aspects of sustainability.

What is sustainability?

The history of humanity's relationship with the natural environment, at least in the West, can be summarised in one word: domination. The natural environment has been seen as a source of food and raw materials all to be placed in the service of human projects. Where the natural environment gets in the way of such projects, we simply blast our way through, rather like the blasting of a cutting or a tunnel through a hill that has the misfortune to lie in the path of a new motorway. The trouble is, there are now so many of us, and our tools are so powerful, that we are no longer simply blasting a few holes in the natural environment; we are changing the whole fabric of the complex ecosystem of which, in the end, we are just one part.

Rachael Carson was one of the first to see human activity as problematic for the natural environment and to call for a change in the relationship:

> The history of life on earth has been a history of interaction between living things and their surroundings. To a large extent, the physical form and the habits of the earth's vegetation and its animal life have been molded by the environment. Considering the whole span of earthly time, the opposite effect, in which life actually modifies its surroundings, has been relatively slight. Only within the moment of time represented by the present [twenieth] century has one species – man – acquired significant power to alter the nature of his world.
>
> (Carson 2002, p. 5)

Her book *Silent Spring*, originally published in 1962, tells the story of how a chemical (DDT) used to control insects like mosquitos had entered the food chain, leading to catastrophic unforeseen effects on other forms of life, including birds. The then widespread and rather indiscriminate use of DDT is a good example of humans working in 'domination' mode.

Silent Spring was one of the catalysts for a spreading awareness of and concern for the natural environment. Twenty-five years later, this concern prompted the establishment of a UN World Commission on Environment and Development (known as the Brundtland Commission, after its Chair, Gro Harlem Brundtland). Its report, *Our Common Future*, defines *sustainable development* as follows:

> Sustainable development is development that meets the needs of the present without compromising the ability of future generations to meet their own needs.
> (United Nations 1987, Chapter 2, para. 1)

> At a minimum, sustainable development must not endanger the natural systems that support life on Earth: the atmosphere, the waters, the soils, and the living beings.
> (United Nations 1987, Chapter 2, para. 9)

The report also underlines the inseparable link that sustainability requires between the natural environment, economic development and social justice. For example, economic growth is often cited as essential for the elimination of poverty. But a good deal of poverty could be eliminated through a more equitable distribution of existing resources, rather than through growth *per se*. Similarly, environmental concerns are sometimes seen as a luxury that can be afforded once a certain level of economic development is reached. This kind of view overlooks the dependency of economic growth on the natural environment. For just one example, consider the depletion of fish stocks in many parts of the world: the massive (economic) growth in large-scale mechanised fishing has led to a reduction in fish that may never be recovered. Once the fish are gone, there will not be much 'growth' in the fishing industry (see Chapter 5 for more discussion of this issue).

Clearly, then, sustainability is important and it is also complex. But why should mathematics teachers be interested? Well, mathematics is both an important tool in understanding sustainability issues, and is implicated in the causes of environmental degradation, as discussed in the rest of this chapter. As mathematics teachers, we have an opportunity to introduce sustainability issues, and the related role of mathematics, to our students.

The mathematics of sustainability

Mathematics is central to our understanding of human society and the planetary ecosystem. Without mathematics, it would be difficult to go beyond specific local observations to build a bigger picture. We might observe changes in our locality – a river seems to have fewer fish, for example – but it would be difficult to know if these changes were happening elsewhere or if they were part of broader trends. In some cases, it is only through mathematics that most of us have any knowledge of the issue at all. The widespread concern about the Antarctic ozone hole, for example, was prompted by the publication of measurements made by satellites; it could not have been prompted by direct personal experience, since no one can actually *see* the ozone hole.

In general, mathematics is used to understand the world in three ways: description, prediction and communication. The mathematics of *description* includes measurement and statistics. Consider human population as an example. To understand the human population of the planet, it first needs to be described. Individual countries conduct censuses, which lead to reasonably accurate counts of the number of people for that country. These counts can then be combined to come up with a global total (see Table 1.1), although, since population is constantly changing, such totals are

Table 1.1 Estimated mid-year population by major area and region, 2009 and 2010 (population in thousands)

	2009	2010
World	6,817,737	6,895,889
Africa	999,045	1,022,234
Eastern Africa	315,865	324,044
Middle Africa	123,452	126,689
Northern Africa	205,920	209,459
Southern Africa	57,293	57,780
Western Africa	296,515	304,261
Asia	4,120,815	4,164,252
Eastern Asia	1,567,045	1,573,970
South-central Asia	1,740,110	1,764,872
South-eastern Asia	586,803	593,415
Western Asia	226,856	231,995
Europe	736,855	738,199
Eastern Europe	295,241	294,771
Northern Europe	98,619	99,205
Southern Europe	154,364	155,171
Western Europe	188,630	189,052
Latin America and the Caribbean	583,547	590,082
Caribbean	41,362	41,646
Central America	153,746	155,881
South America	388,440	392,555
Northern America	341,490	344,529
Oceania	35,984	36,593
Australia/New Zealand	26,225	26,637
Melanesia	8,560	8,748
Micronesia	532	536
Polynesia	667	673

Source: United Nations, Department of Economic and Social Affairs, Population Division (2011)

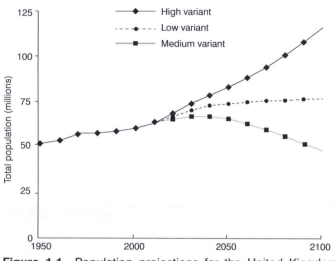

Figure 1.1 Population projections for the United Kingdom based on probabilistic projections of total fertility from the 2010 Revision (United Nations 2011: 918)

always approximate. In many cases, averages are used and population data might include, for example, the proportion of the population in different age groups. As this proportion varies from place to place, the proportion is an average.

The mathematics of *prediction* is often more complex, involving the identification of trends and the construction and use of mathematical models. Various models are available, for example, to predict how the population of the planet will change over the coming decades. These models are based, in part, on analysis of past changes, as well as current information about things like birth rates and death rates. The models include certain assumptions. In the case of population, the models include the assumption that economic development will lead to declining fertility rates; that is, people in richer countries have fewer children. The chart shown in Figure 1.1 shows UN projections for the population of the UK. These projections are based on some quite advanced mathematics, including Bayesian statistics. Note that the projections include a range of scenarios, some more likely than others.

Finally, the mathematics of *communication* includes mathematical and statistical literacy. This literacy is apparent in the production and consumption of scientific information. In order to communicate their findings, scientists may make use of, for example, tables, charts and graphs. The form of this information varies according to the audience: a scientific report will look different from an article in a newspaper or a television news report. Equally, the consumers of this information also need mathematical or statistical literacy, needing to have the skills and know-how for interpreting and evaluating different kinds of charts, tables or statistics. Consider the mathematical literacy involved in interpreting the population information shown in Table 1.1 or the projections shown in Figure 1.1. The internet is awash with data, some of it of dubious validity. Mathematical literacy includes some critical sense of what counts as useful, reliable information.

Mathematics, then, is vital in describing different aspects of our world, from fish stocks to forest fires. More advanced mathematics is used to model and predict future trends. Such predictions are important for planning and development. Finally, mathematics is necessary to communicate and interpret information about our world. The important role of mathematics in understanding global sustainability raises the question of how mathematics teaching should take this role into account.

Mathematics teaching and sustainability

Teaching mathematics as if the planet matters goes beyond the purpose commonly ascribed to mathematics teaching of producing numerate citizens, suitably equipped with enough mathematical know-how to enter the labour market. Environmental problems like climate change, deforestation or pollution are complex and understanding them involves a good deal of mathematics. Furthermore, such problems are not laboratory science, given that they are embedded in the fabric of our society. Tackling them will increasingly require our participation, which in turn suggests that education could (or should) prepare students to contribute, not only as possible future scientists, but also as citizens. To consider how mathematics teaching can take on this role, it might help to say something about how education in general can engage with sustainability.

Renert (2011) summarises three levels or stages in educational approaches to sustainability: accommodation, reformation and transformation. An *accommodation* approach tends to focus on passing on knowledge. For example, students might learn about the types of pollution emitted by cars. The knowledge to be learned is clearly established and presented, perhaps in a textbook, and is based on a belief in the efficacy of science and mathematics to understand and explain the world and solve problems. A *reformation* approach promotes a degree of critical thinking, inviting students to consider values as well as knowledge and to think about ways to make the world better, without necessarily questioning underlying assumptions. Students might, for example, consider whether car emissions are good or bad and think about how they might be reduced. A *transformation* approach, however, focuses much more on the nature of knowledge and its relation to action, including the sense that what we know and how we act depends on who and where we are. In such an approach, students interested in car pollution might examine where emissions data come from, generate their own data and take action in response. From this perspective, sustainable development *is* a form of learning. These three approaches are progressively more challenging. The boundaries between them are not clear, so it may be better to think of them as points on a continuum.

These different approaches help to suggest different approaches to teaching mathematics as if the planet mattered (see Table 1.2). An approach based on accommodation would be focused mostly on teaching mathematical facts and procedures. The outside world would only arise as a context for mathematical tasks, as used, for example, in 'real world' word problems. In these kinds of problems, the nature of the context is not especially important. A survey on car use could just as easily be a survey on favourite ice-cream flavours. The contexts are just a way of presenting mathematics. An approach based on reformation would include more attention to mathematical thinking, critical thinking and problem solving. In this

Table 1.2 Incorporating sustainability into mathematics education

Transformation	Teaching and learning mathematics to analyse and critique the perspectives that shape how the world is understood and engage in action to change the world	Outside world as origin of sustainability problems, for which mathematics may be one tool (or part of the problem)
Reformation	Teaching and learning mathematics to relate mathematics to the world and to refine how things are done	Outside world as origin of mathematics problems
Accommodation	Teaching and learning mathematical facts and procedures	Outside world used as a way of presenting mathematics

approach, the outside world could provide the basis for mathematics problems. For example, concern about pollution levels around a school could provide a starting point for a survey on car use in the school neighbourhood. At the end of the day, however, the purpose of the activity is still to learn about conducting surveys and using statistics, as set out in the curriculum. By contrast, an approach to mathematics teaching based on transformation starts with sustainability. Mathematics is not seen as a definitive way to solve problems, but as a tool with limitations and constraints. From such a perspective, concern about pollution could lead to a campaign for a car-free neighbourhood. The campaign would involve a variety of actions, including interviewing, surveying, and collecting and critiquing publicly available data. The resulting work could be presented to school governors or local councillors. It would also involve students reflecting on and changing their own actions; for example, organising themselves to walk safely to school. The point here is that mathematics is present, but in the service of sustainability, rather than as an end in itself. For Renert (2011), such an approach would, therefore, ultimately involve the transformation of mathematics teaching, not just the transformation of the outside world.

These ideas have echoes in approaches to mathematics motivated by a concern for social justice. Gutstein (2006), for example, worked as a teacher in Chicago. Many of his students were Spanish-speaking Latinos or Latinas. In his teaching, he used what he called 'Real-World Projects' to encourage his students to think critically about social issues, using mathematics to do so. At the start of the school year in 2002, for example, a year after the September 11 attacks, students in a class of 12–13-year-olds had many questions and concerns about the attacks. One student had a brother who had joined the navy. Gutstein asked her if her brother would have joined the navy if he could go to university for free. She said that he would not. This exchange led to a real-world project called 'The cost of the B-2 bomber – where do our tax dollars go?':

> The essence of the project was to use US Department of Defense data and find the cost for one B-2 bomber, then compare it to a four-year, full scholarship to

the University of Wisconsin-Madison, a prestigious out-of-state university. The students had to answer whether the whole graduating class of the neighborhood high school (about 250 students) could receive the four-year, full scholarships for the cost of one bomber. Eventually, they discovered that the cost of one bomber could pay for the full, four-year scholarships for the whole graduating class (assuming constant size and costs) for the next 79 years!

(Gutstein 2006: 3)

This project, which was carefully structured through a series of questions and sources of information (see Gutstein 2006: 246–7), exemplifies what Gutstein calls teaching mathematics for social justice:

in which real and potentially controversial issues were explored and discussed; genuine views (including my own) and differences were solicited, accepted, and respected; and mathematics became a key analytical tool with which to investigate, make sense out of, and possibly take action on important social justice issues in the world.

(Gutstein 2006: 3)

This approach has much in common with the transformational perspective mentioned above, although with a focus on social justice rather than environmental or sustainability issues. What they share is a sense that the outside world can be more than a rather contrived way to dress up a mathematics problem. Instead, mathematics becomes a tool to understand issues of interest and importance to students and to society more generally. Moreover, such approaches go beyond simply making mathematics 'relevant'. Gutstein is quite explicit in his desire to challenge students' thinking about society. Using this kind of approach in the classroom can be engaging and empowering for our students (and potentially 'dangerous', given that 'it encourages people to think, and possibly, to act', Stocker 2006: 11). What is perhaps missing from these ideas is some attention to the role of mathematics itself in society. Those B-2 bombers, for example, involve a good deal of mathematics in their design and construction.

Critical mathematics education and the 'formatting power' of mathematics in a technological society

Critical mathematics education, as developed by Skovsmose (1984, 1994, 2009), starts by thinking about the role of mathematics in society. At the start of this chapter, I pointed out how mathematics is used to describe, predict and communicate the science of sustainability. These uses, however, are all rather instrumental examples of using mathematics as a tool to understand the world. Similarly, in Gutstein's teaching of mathematics for social justice, students are encouraged to use mathematics as a tool to explore social issues. Skovsmose, however, emphasises the role of mathematics itself in *creating* our world. As a result, he argues that mathematics teaching can include a critical analysis of this role. Mathematics is not simply a powerful way of interrogating the world around us, it is part of the structure of our society. A critical mathematics education offers students some insight into how mathematics is part of their lives and the consequences it can have. In this section and the next, these ideas are developed in more depth.

The idea that mathematics shapes our world and our lives can be summarised in three main points. First, we live in a technological society. In particular, we make use of and are increasingly dependent on information technology through the widespread use of computers. Many of us have personal computers or mobile phones and use the internet for shopping and communication, but information technology is much more widespread than this. Your washing machine, your car and your central heating all depend on information technology, in the form of microprocessors that control their operation and provide the interface between you and the machine. Beyond this, road and rail networks, the electricity grid, the health service, finance, medicine, education and government are all dependent on information technology systems. These systems are part of how we seek to dominate the natural environment, whether in the service of transportation, energy production, disease control or the many other ways in which we exploit the ecosystems on which we depend.

The second point is that all this information technology involves a lot of mathematics. The control systems in your washing machine are mathematical. The security systems in your mobile phone are mathematical. But most of all, mathematics is needed to model different parts of the world so that the technology can operate on them. Modelling here refers to the process of mathematising aspects of the world in order to solve problems, a process akin to translating from human experience to mathematical terms. Skovsmose gives a nice example: when you book a flight, you interact with an IT-based booking system. This booking system records who has booked seats on different flights, lets you know which seats are still available and calculates the cost of different available seats. To do all this, the software includes various mathematical models. These models mathematise the airline network and include, as variables, the times of day and year of flights, the popularity of the route and current sales. This model creates a kind of representation of the airline network, although it also leaves out quite a lot, including the effects of airline travel on the environment.

The third point is that the mathematics embedded in information technology has tangible social effects. The mathematics does not simply describe the world, it changes it. Skovsmose calls this idea the *formatting power* of mathematics. To illustrate, he discusses the phenomenon of flight overbooking. When you arrive for your flight and the airline has sold too many tickets, some passengers are not able to fly. Mathematical models of airline ticket sales deliberately include a degree of overbooking, since a proportion of passengers with tickets do not show up for their flight. The airline wants the plane to be as full as possible, so they aim to compensate for these missing passengers. The booking model therefore includes parameters that take into account the variables mentioned above such as, perhaps, flights to holiday destinations have fewer no shows than a primarily business route, or flights in the morning might have fewer no shows than flights in the afternoon. The model, however, which is probabilistic, is imprecise and consequently sometimes there are too many passengers and the flight is oversold. This example illustrates how mathematics is a powerful predictive tool, but also shows how this tool has limitations and real social effects: some people are not able to fly. These limitations are unavoidable. Mathematics formalises a situation, effectively creating a particular mathematical interpretation, which in turn develops a social reality of its own. The mathematical models are not necessarily good or bad. For instance, airline ticket-sales models contribute to convenience and in some cases to cheaper fares. The model does, however, change the nature of pricing and of air travel itself. In Skovsmose's (2001) terms, 'mathematics itself becomes part of reality and inseparable from other aspects of society' (p. 11).

The formatting power of mathematics is directly relevant to issues of sustainability. Here is one example and you will find others throughout the book:

- *Flooding*: In recent years, Britain has been plagued by river flooding. But how did houses come to be built in areas prone to flooding? This issue is complex, with factors like climate change making it more challenging. Mathematical models play a key role. Local authorities use mathematical models to predict river flow. Based on these predictions, they develop planning policies (where to build) and construct flood defences. In some cases, the models may omit key factors such as increased flash flooding due to climate change or changing river flows due to dredging or silting. Models may suggest some areas are not at risk but, over time, the risk increases and flooding may occur.

The embedding of mathematics within information technology has a number of significant consequences. One is that the mathematics is, in some sense, invisible. Interacting with software or IT systems does not generally give users access to the mathematical algorithms and models on which the system is based. This invisibility, of course, makes the system work more efficiently, but it also masks the role of mathematics and with it the human decisions that are made about which variables and parameters to include. Finally, information technology means that a mathematical 'view' of our world is deeply embedded in our society. Only things that can be measured and modelled can be included. A critical mathematics education, then, will include some attention to the formatting power of mathematics and the invisible role of mathematics in our lives.

Three forms of knowing

To delineate more clearly how critical mathematics education might work, Skovsmose (1994: 98–102) discusses three forms of knowing: mathematical knowing, technological knowing and reflective knowing. *Mathematical knowing* is concerned with formal mathematics, the symbolic system and logical relations that make up abstract mathematics. *Technological knowing* is about the application of mathematics, knowing both how to construct a tool and how to use it. Mathematical modelling is one such tool. Knowing how to construct a model requires more than a familiarity with, for example, different types of equations. It requires an understanding of how to construct particular equations to model a situation, as well as an understanding of how to use the model. *Reflective knowing* concerns meta-level awareness of the broader effects of mathematics, of its social or ethical consequences. The key distinction between technological knowing and reflective knowing is that technological knowing 'is insufficient for predicting and analysing the results and consequences of its own production; reflections building upon different competencies are needed' (p. 99). That is, mathematics is not enough if you want to understand the consequences of, for example, a model of river flow. Skovsmose gives a useful example:

> Let us, as an example, look at the problem of motoring. Too many (private) cars cause pollution. This form of transport carries some serious risks (of an ecological nature, for instance) the consequences of which we are going to face in the not-too-distant future. The way to confront these emerging problems is not to develop the driver's driving skills [...], nor is it to give the driver more information about mechanics – how the car is actually constructed, how the brakes work, how they can be repaired, and so on. Naturally, it is useful both to be able to repair a car and to drive it in a better way, but this is not a satisfactory answer to the problem of motoring presented. To face this problem and to react to it in an adequate way, we have to develop a better understanding of motoring, seen as the complex phenomenon of organising transport and traffic in general. What are the economical and ecological consequences of motoring? What social and political actions are needed and which seem to be possible?
>
> (Skovsmose 1994: 98)

Knowing how to drive and knowing how a car is made are metaphors for mathematical and technological knowing respectively. These forms of knowing are insufficient to understand the effects of motor transport. For that, a different form of knowing is required. Of course, to understand the effects of motor transport, it helps to know how people drive and how cars are made. There is a link. But only reflective knowing involves a broader perspective, often missing in school mathematics. Reflective knowing, for Skovsmose, is the basis for critical mathematics education, the project of which is the empowerment of critical citizens.

Skvosmose (1994: 106-114) proposes three related foci for reflective knowing, all of which are about developing a better understanding of the role of mathematics in shaping our lives and our world. First, reflective knowing can focus on the purposes of the modelling process. These purposes influence how the model is developed as well as how it is used. The models used in airline booking systems, for example, presumably have strongly commercial purposes. Models of river flow may have political or economic purposes. These purposes are not apparent in the models themselves; the language of mathematics is perceived to be neutral, so that issues of power, for example, are not apparent. Reflective knowing can focus on these purposes to consider, among other things, whose interests a particular model serves.

Reflective knowing can also focus on the process of translating a problem or situation into mathematical form. Like all translations, the process is inexact. In the case of mathematics, the uncertainties and imprecisions of the world are formalised. But the process also introduces uncertainties. In mathematising a situation, it is not possible to include values or prejudices, for example. As suggested already, airline-booking models do not include the environmental effects of flying or the broader societal effects of widespread affordable air travel. As in the example of motoring, the booking models are only narrowly concerned with a specific aspect of flying. Reflective knowing needs to examine the broader consequences.

Finally, reflective knowing can focus on the formatting power of mathematics. It can focus not just on how mathematics represents reality, but on how it becomes reality. If your house is built on a flood plain, and it floods, you have perhaps experienced the formatting power of mathematics.

In the context of sustainability, reflective knowing can lead to awareness of the way in which mathematics constructs our environment, including the following points:

- How mathematising systems like the climate, the economy or society involves human beings making decisions about what is important to include and what can be left out. Economic models, for example, often ignore environmental costs.
- How these ostensibly mathematical decisions may reflect the political or economic interests of the people constructing the model. For example, in the Gulf of Mexico oil spill of 2010, estimates of both the quantity of oil and the financial costs to BP were consistently underestimated.
- How mathematics can bring an illusion of control over our environment and how mathematics has limitations. For example, the construction of flood defences based on models of such variables as rainfall, river flow and absorption has a feeling of mathematical rigour that is of little use when the defences fail.

Implications for teaching mathematics

This chapter has discussed some approaches to teaching mathematics as part of sustainability and has looked at the mathematical basis of our technological society. These ideas suggest some general directions for mathematics teachers interested in working on sustainability. In particular, mathematics teaching might aim to develop a transformative approach that, in addition to mathematical and technological knowing, also fosters reflective knowing. In the first part of this book, we consider in a little more depth what such an approach might look like, focusing on five topics that are closely connected with the general issue of sustainability. These topics are: economic growth; climate change; food; biodiversity; and human rights and social justice.

In each chapter, we examine some of the mathematics that is usually invisible in discussion of such issues. The chapter on climate change, for example, examines some of the mathematics involved in demonstrating that the climate has become warmer in recent years. We have selected mathematics that falls within the range of secondary school mathematics curricula, although for this first part of the book, there is no direct attempt to address specific curriculum topics. Our aim, with these first chapters, is to illustrate how issues related to global sustainability involve some accessible mathematics, and that this mathematics can lead to a deeper and more critical understanding of the issues in question. Along the way, each chapter includes brief suggestions for how reformation-based or transformation-based approaches teaching ideas could be developed. We hope that our treatment of these issues will prompt readers to pursue their own more extended mathematical explorations and will prompt teachers to develop suitable sustainability-oriented mathematics lessons or units to incorporate into their teaching.

Further reading

- If you found the population example in this chapter interesting, you might like to look at *National Geographic* magazine. The theme of the January 2011 edition is 'Population 7 Billion' and throughout 2011 the magazine includes articles on population-related topics. See: http://ngm.nationalgeographic.com/2011/01/table-of-contents.
- For more global and country-specific population statistics, see the United Nations Statistics Division, which publishes regular 'Population and Vital Statistics Reports' on global population: http://unstats.un.org/unsd/demographic/products/vitstats/default.htm and http://unstats.un.org/unsd/demographic/products/dyb/dyb2009.htm.
- The Brundtland Report is quite readable and can be found online at: http://www.un-documents.net/wced-ocf.htm.
- *Silent Spring* (Carson, 2002) is also very readable and its broader argument remains relevant.

References

Carson, R. (2002) *Silent Spring* (originally published 1962). New York: Houghton Mifflin.

Gutstein, E. (2006) *Reading and Writing the World with Mathematics: Toward a Pedagogy for Social Justice,* New York: Routledge.

Renert, M. (2011) Mathematics for life: sustainable mathematics education, *For the Learning of Mathematics,* 31(1) 20–6.

Skovsmose, O. (1984) Mathematical education and democracy, *Educational Studies in Mathematics,* 21: 109–28.

Skovsmose, O. (1994) *Towards a Philosophy of Critical Mathematics Education,* Dordrecht: Kluwer.

Skovsmose, O. (2001) Mathematics in action: a challenge for social theorising. In E. Simmt, and B. Davis (eds) *Proceedings of the 2001 annual meeting of the Canadian Mathematics Education Study Group.* Edmonton, AB: CMESG.

Skovsmose, O. (2009) *In Doubt: About Language, Mathematics, Knowledge and Life-worlds,* Rotterdam: Sense Publishers.

United Nations (1987) *Our Common Future: World Commission on Environment and Development.* Oxford: Oxford University Press.

United Nations, Department of Economic and Social Affairs, Population Division (2011) *World Population Prospects: The 2010 Revision* (CD-ROM Edition). New York: UN.

The economy

Laurinda Brown

Although this chapter is entitled 'The economy', the issue for the planet at the moment of writing is 'growth' and the question of whether economic development is reaching planetary limits. Adverts tempt us to buy a bigger car, replace our clothes with more fashionable items before the ones we already have wear out, and many people eat more than is good for them, leading to rates of diabetes and obesity growing. Recently (in 2012), assumptions about growth in gross domestic product (GDP), wages and profits from dealing in stocks and shares have been brought into question, globally, by failure of the banks, double-dip recessions and possibilities of depression in the UK. What do these words mean? There are definitions later in the chapter. What happened? What is the role of mathematics in the workings of an economy? Using the idea of the formatting power of mathematics from Chapter 1, the economy is an area in which mathematics plays a role in creating the social conditions of our world. Are there examples of the translation of human experience to mathematical terms and even the formatting power of mathematics embedded within the recent crises? This chapter aims to explore the idea of growth, finding out where it has come from and exploring different models including those suggested for a sustainable future.

Alongside any colloquial meaning, 'growth' is a mathematical concept. What does five per cent growth per annum mean to you? What does it look like when drawn on a graph? Starting with £100, say, linear growth would be equivalent to adding £5 to the pot each year. The graph would be a straight line, $y = 5x + 100$, where y is the total amount saved after x years. Linear growth has a constant rate of change, the function increasing in a controlled and predictable way. It is more usual, however, that five per cent growth per annum means something else. At the end of the first year, adding the £5 to the original capital of £100 gives £105 from which you would then calculate the five per cent interest in the second year and so on. This is exponential growth, still predictable, but exploding into unimaginably sized amounts over time. Although five per cent growth per annum feels linear, in fact, whilst the growth is slow at the start and for a short time the exponential function can be modelled linearly, over time the two sets of figures diverge dramatically.

To give a sense of just how quickly the exponential function grows, there is an old story about a king being given a chessboard by a subject with the request that the king give one grain of rice for the first square and double the grains of rice for each of the other squares in turn. Would you agree to this exchange? The function is exponential because the pattern is $y = 2^{x-1}$ where y is the number of grains of rice on the xth square. The first square has $2^{1-1} = 2^0 = 1$ grain, the second square has $2^{2-1} = 2^1 = 2$ grains. Continuing with the following sequence 4, 8, 16, 32, 64, 128, 256, 512 and we are only on the tenth square! By which square would the king have to produce 1,000,000 grains of rice? It is unlikely that the king would have enough grains of rice to complete the contract. What would the total number of grains of rice be?

The following story, apparently a French riddle for children (Meadows, *et al.* 1972: 29, credited to Robert Lattes), gives a cautionary tale when dealing with exponentials related to a moral of the need to act earlier than you think. A water lily grows on a pond, doubling in size each day. If its growth is unchecked it will completely cover the pond in 30 days, choking off the other forms of life in the water. For a long time the plant seems small, so you decide not to worry about cutting it back until it covers half the pond. On what day will the water lily cover half the pond?

The doubling time for the lily is one day. £100 left in the bank at five per cent growth per annum will double in 14 years. Doubling is a useful idea when dealing with exponentials to give a sense of growth over time. Look at different percentage growth rates per annum and their doubling times. What is the relationship?

Perspectives on growth

Surely we need growth? Or do we? In this section, there are illustrations of conceptualising growth from three perspectives that question this need. Initially, population doubling from a geographical perspective, followed by the Royal Society of Arts' president's views and, finally, through the voice of Iain M. Banks discussing science fiction literature.

Perspective 1 – Geographical: In January 2011, the *National Geographic* had the arresting front cover headline *Population 7 Billion: How your world will change*. This was written over a background photograph of Shanghai, which had a population of 14 million people, 2.3 million vehicles and 9,320 miles of roads. How many years before the population will double again from the 7 billion in 2011? To answer this question, you would need a mathematical model and some assumptions (see Chapter 9 for a fuller discussion of mathematical modelling). There are more than twice as many people on the planet now as in 1960, when there were an estimated 3 billion people. The population doubled between 1950 and 1987 (2.5 to 5 billion), 1956 and 1994 (2.8 to 5.6 billion) and 1960 and 1998 (3 to 6 billion), giving a relatively stable rate of growth of population of between 1.8 and 1.9 per cent (Hern 1999: 70). What would current growth rates be? As the population increases, there needs to be growth in everything from food production to housing stock. Or does there? What about limiting growth such as through political interference with number of children allowed per family (China is already below replacement fertility, thanks in part to its coercive one-child policy, Kunzig 2011: 49) or quotas for food and water supply?

Perspective 2 – Royal Society of Arts' President's views: David Attenborough (2011), in a lecture entitled 'People and Planet', discusses 'the fundamental truth that Malthus proclaimed … There cannot be more people on this earth than can be fed.' This statement raises questions such as: what does it mean for a person to be fed? How have farming methods changed so that there is more food produced by farmers for the same amount of land? How much food is wasted? David Attenborough, when thinking about 'sustainable growth', quoted Kenneth Boulding, President Kennedy's environmental advisor, who said, 45 years ago, 'anyone who believes in indefinite growth in anything physical, on a physically finite planet is either mad – or an economist' (Attenborough 2011).

Perspective 3 – Iain M. Banks, discussing science fiction literature: When reading science fiction as a child or young adult, Iain Banks (1994) the author (who writes science fiction under the name Iain M. Banks) was struck that whilst the technology was more sophisticated and in general authors projected themselves into a differently organised future, the one thing that seemed to stay the same was the thinking behind futuristic economics. There was money and wealth, the haves and the have-nots. He set out to change this in his series of novels around 'The Culture'. This world presupposes that the creation of a planned economy (rather than market forces) had happened some time in the past and had evolved into a culture based on the idea of a 'minimally wasteful elegance', a 'kind of galactic ecological awareness allied to a desire to create beauty and goodness' (Banks 1994). Here the economy is indistinguishable from society.

Banks's (1994) perspective, whilst galactic ecological awareness seems a long way away from present-day reality, could act as a motivation to support a belief that alternative visions of society are possible. However, arguments against growth are, of course, contested and one counter-argument runs that growth can proceed through ever greater gains in efficiency and productivity, even on a finite planet.

Limits to growth?

In 1972, a report for the Club of Rome's project on the predicament of mankind was published called *The Limits to Growth* (Meadows *et al.* 1972). Thirty years later, three of the original four authors published *Limits to Growth, the 30-year update* (Meadows *et al.* 2004). Relatively quickly after publication of the original book, the statistics for such important aspects as, say, non-renewable natural resources (pp. 56–9) were not as bad as had been predicted. For instance, as commodities became scarcer and prices rose, alternatives were found and there was a shift in population growth figures given that the average birth rate dropped faster than the death rate (Meadows *et al.* 2004: 28), lengthening the doubling time. From our current perspective, however, the questions that were being posed were good ones. With the growth of population still being exponential, even with the lower growth rate the 'net number of people added to the planet was in fact higher in 2000 than it was in 1965' (Meadows *et al.* 2004: 29). The factors that led to divergence between the predicted figures in the original *Limits to Growth* and what actually happened were related to individual creativity (for example, the 'invention in 1976 of the pop-top opener tab on the aluminium soda can meant that the tab stayed with the can, therefore passing back through the recycling process, rather than being thrown away' (Meadows *et al.* 2004: 103)), and some economists believe that new technologies will solve issues such as water and mineral shortages for us. One background mathematical idea behind all these discussions, which is rarely made explicit, is how we measure economic growth.

Gross domestic product (GDP)

GDP is 'the most commonly used single measure of a country's overall economic activity. It represents the total value at constant prices of final goods and services produced within a country during a specified time period, such as one year' (IMF 2012). Think for a moment about how you would set about calculating this figure. It is not surprising, perhaps, that there are a variety of methods, all based on different assumptions and differing models that should, in theory at least, give similar results. For instance, the expenditure method gives:

$$GDP = C + I + G + (X\text{--}M)$$

where C stands for private consumption; I, gross investment; G, government spending; X is gross exports; and M, gross imports.

In contrast, the income method gives:

$$GDP = E + P + (T\text{--}S)$$

where E stands for the total of wages, salaries, and social security; P is made up of the sum of profits from big firms and small businesses; and $(T\text{--}S)$ stands for tax revenues less subsidies on production and imports.

These calculations are based on the actual goods and services within a country. However, once the concept of GDP exists and has a value, independent of the actual goods and services from which that value was calculated, it takes on a life of its own.

The formulas for GDP are a translation of human experience into mathematical terms; however, what happens next is an example of the formatting power of mathematics. The International Monetary Fund (IMF 2012), for instance, measures growth in GDP and compares figures between nations, publishing predictions for each country's growth. These figures in turn can be used as some sort of measure of economic health. Mathematical techniques applied to raw GDP data are used to make comparisons meaningful both for comparisons of GDP over time within one country and comparison of GDP between countries:

■ Comparison of raw GDP data for one country over time needs to take into account factors such as the value of the currency in which the GDP was calculated over time, accounting for any inflation or deflation. So, for year-to-year comparisons, the so-called real GDP figure is used.

■ Comparison between countries leads to the idea of GDP per capita (where total GDP is divided by the resident population on a given date, both citizens and any immigrants). Again, there are alternative ways of creating a value that could be compared, such as GDP per citizen (total GDP divided by the numbers of citizens resident in the country on a given date). How similar would these figures be in different countries? What factors would lead to divergence or convergence of the two figures?

Maps, charts and tables of real GDP growth across the globe with, currently, predictions of the state of the world up to 2017 (IMF 2012) give a sense of truth to what is effectively a model resulting in a set of numbers. Patterns are interesting to observe such as the nations with accelerated growth compared to those with stagnant or even negative growth. (The website www.gapminder.org has visualisation of the growth of national incomes over time.) It is easy to fall into the trap of accelerated growth, good, slow or negative growth, bad and yet, what different models might there be for measuring growth? At the microeconomic level there are laws of supply and demand where there are limits to growth. Individual businesses do not grow indefinitely because of constraints such as storage space; the weather (an extended drought can put umbrella manufacturers out of business!); rising costs of transportation of goods through the rising price of oil might lead to limiting supply because the rising price puts a brake on demand (see Figure 2.1).

There is also a law of supply that says that the higher price, the higher the quantity supplied (the general rule is that quantities supplied move in the same

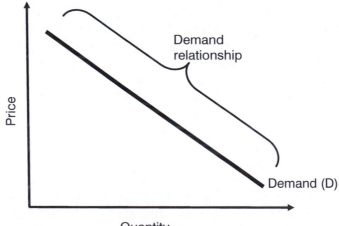

Figure 2.1 The law of demand states that, if all other factors remain equal, the higher the price of a good, the less people will demand that good. Read more at: http://www.investopedia.com/university/economics/economics3.asp/#ixzz2303B6yXg

directions as changes in price). This feels counter-intuitive perhaps. Think of it this way: manufacturers increase production given the high price to increase their profits. However, this means that for a prestige item, the supply must be kept down to keep up the high price. For example, around the time of the global financial crisis, car manufacturers in Australia had an oversupply of large vehicles that they could not shift. The manufacturers got it wrong. The demand for family station wagons went down because of the increasing cost of fuel and families beginning to tighten their budgets. The families now wanted a small- to medium-sized vehicle and these were in underproduction. The suppliers then had to discount the larger cars. Since the crisis, some suppliers now produce large cars on demand. The orders come first, supplied just-in-time. The suppliers do not want to have to discount the price below the cost of production. There are checks and balances in the system and equilibrium is when supply equals demand. What would this graph look like?

At the macroeconomic level, however, since the 1940s when the idea of GDP arose out of World War II and the Great Depression (Dickinson 2011), the assumption has been that growth of real GDP, considered to be a measure of a country's overall welfare, can continue to rise without limit even if there are occasional setbacks. These setbacks were considered to be a normal part of the business cycle, the boom and bust that Gordon Brown said there would be no return to when he was Chancellor of the Exchequer of the UK (Summers 2008). Graphs of GDP over time in a country make for interesting data for predicting future growth (again, see more activities linked to modelling in Chapter 9).

Interlude: definitions of recession, depression and related ideas

This interlude acts as a break between the discussion of growth and the second half of the chapter where there is a case study of the formatting power of mathematics followed by instructions to play the Trading Game. Given the previous discussion, the meanings of words like recession should be more transparent.

Recession is defined as two consecutive quarters of negative economic growth measured by a country's GDP. There is decline in activity across the economy lasting longer than a few months. We have recently experienced the global recession of 2008–2009, which brought a great amount of attention to the risky investment strategies used by many large financial institutions, along with the truly global nature of the financial system. As a result of such a widespread global recession, the economies of virtually all the world's developed and developing nations suffered extreme setbacks and numerous government policies were implemented to help prevent a similar future financial crisis. A recession generally lasts from six to eighteen months, and interest rates usually fall during these months to stimulate the economy. When interest rates fall, those with variable interest rate mortgages, for example, experience relief as funds are freed back to the household budget. This may encourage discretionary spending on items such as eating out, entertainment, electronics and travel, which were areas where cutbacks had previously been made. Lower interest rates signal that it is a good time to spend and are intended to build consumer confidence. There are cheap rates at which to borrow money and less reward for saving.

Double-dip recession is when GDP growth slides back to negative after a quarter or two of positive growth. A double-dip recession refers to a recession followed by a short-lived recovery, followed by another recession.

Depression is a severe and prolonged recession characterised by inefficient economic productivity, high unemployment and falling price levels. In times of depression, consumers' confidence and investments decrease, which can then provoke further reductions in economic activity in a potentially vicious cycle. The classic example of this occurred in the 1930s, when the Great Depression shook the global economy. (This section is paraphrased from http://www.investopedia.com. Many of the terms discussed are illustrated with a related video. When you get to the site, simply search for the term you want to have explained and you will be taken to the relevant section of the site.)

Students could be asked to explore these terms in relation to the performance of their own economy since 1940, perhaps or over the period 2000 to 2010 around the latest crash. Was there anything different in GDP rates leading up to, or following, the crash of 2008 compared to other recessions (see Guardian Datablog 2009)?

An example of the formatting power of mathematics: risk and the Black–Scholes equation

Once upon a time, when the idea of GDP was young, banks were careful about risk. To get a loan to take out a mortgage, there were rules that linked income to size of loan. For example, there were gendered assumptions such as when a young couple, both in employment, wished to take out the loan, perhaps only 1.5 times the man's salary would be considered because the woman might go on maternity leave and stay at home to look after the baby. Wages were lower, but so were house prices and the young couple also needed to save for maybe a 10 per cent deposit on the cost of the house.

Recently, in the UK, people who lived through those times were mystified by stories of no-deposit loans for mortgages and loans for amounts five times the combined salaries of a young couple. How was this possible? There was an awareness of a radical change in how banks and building societies operated but few questioned what was happening, such was the trust in the banks as an institution.

This situation was created by mathematics that few people, even the traders on the floor of stock exchanges around the world, understood. The Black–Scholes equation (not given here because of its complexity, see further reading if you are interested in the actual formula) gave a value to the risk being taken, 'a rational way to price a financial contract when it still had time to run' (Stewart 2012: 18). What traders thought they could do was lay-off risk using Black–Scholes. Although the process of using the equation was based on assumptions and was a difficult calculation, traders used a Black–Scholes's calculating machine that had been given to them, without understanding those assumptions. Lanchester (2010) admits that he also has absolutely no idea what the mathematics means but effectively what the calculation seemed to achieve was taking the risk out of dealing with derivatives, transactions that are agreed for some future time like the wheat harvest, and the now infamous sub-prime (high-risk) mortgages by selling them on. Lanchester's (2010) book is also useful background on why the money markets went for a system that is built on debt rather than assets. The title of his book says it all, *I.O.U: why everyone owes everyone and no-one can pay*. A couple of examples might help this counter-intuitive notion of dealing in debt.

The first example is from Stewart's (2012) article. The phrase 'call option' is used below, which needs some explanation. If you buy a 'call option' you have the right, but not the obligation, to buy goods at a particular price at a particular time. Hence, if you sell a 'call option' you think the goods will not be worth that price when the time comes.

> Alice wants to sell a call option on carrots because she bought it as an investment and the last thing she actually wants to take delivery of is carrots. Bob is thinking of buying it. When the option matures, in 180 days' time, it gives its owner the opportunity to buy a quantity of carrots for $70,000. At the moment, their market value is $100,000. Alice is asking $31,000. Should Bob buy? Bob already knows three key variables: time to maturity ($T = 180$ days), strike price ($K = \$70,000$), and today's market price ($S = \$100,000$). The risk-free interest rate is low: $r = 2\%$. He estimates the volatility (s) of stock in carrots [sic], the underlying asset, by his favourite method, getting 7 per cent. He types these five numbers into a Black–Scholes calculator program, which uses the formulae to work out a 'rational' price. It turns out to be $30,687. Bob declines Alice's offer.
>
> (Lanchester 2010: 18)

What is amazing here is the formatting power of the mathematics that neither Bob nor Alice understands. Remember, nobody actually used the mathematical thinking behind the equations to consider the assumptions on which they were based. The traders simply had a way of calculating that seemed to work for quite a long time.

Another example, paraphrased from Lanchester (2010: 48–9) this time: How is it possible that the basic transaction can spawn many derivative transactions and fortunes in what is called 'notional action'? Granovetter (2005), writing before the crash of 2008, writes about 'innovation in what is considered a marketable commodity' (p. 44), where 'items proscribed at one point in time can later become routine commodities'. For instance, life insurance 'which early nineteenth-century Americans saw as sacrilege, or at best gambling, but which by the late 1800s had established itself as a breadwinner's obligation' (p. 44). The other example discussed by Granovetter is:

> the more recent emergence of financial derivatives as a legitimate product [where again] the perception of options changed from that of dubious gamble to respected financial instrument. [...W]hile in 1970, financial derivatives were so unimportant that no reliable figures could be found for market size, by 2000, the notional value of such contracts worldwide was in excess of $100 trillion (pp. 44–5).

So, the notional action is the value of all derivative contracts generated from the underlying asset. Part of the story of growth of the financial derivatives market is the story of the Black–Scholes formula. Its discovery was a 'defining moment in the mathematisation of the market. Within months, traders were using equations and vocabulary straight out of [the formula] and the worldwide derivatives business took off like a rocket' (Lanchester, 2010: 48). Derivatives are 'products that were designed initially to transfer or hedge risks – to purchase some insurance against the prospect of a price going down when your main bet was that the price would go up' (p. 49). Say you are a pig farmer and you want to sell your next season's pork bellies in advance to ensure a good price. A trader buys them for $100,000 and at this stage we move into derivative trading. These are not deals for the actual bellies but for the derivative of the bellies. The actual price of bellies will move around dependent on the market. So, if the price of pork bellies is rising then the pork belly derivative contract at $100,000 becomes a much sought-after product because I might be able to buy the bellies cheaper than if I paid the going rate. If pork belly prices are going down I might choose to hedge my bets by purchasing some insurance, betting against an even lower price. The notional contracts can spiral far, far away from the underlying real assets and stop being simply about reducing risks but can tempt traders into deals that increase risk and consequent rewards, leading to large losses if the bet does not work.

- Trade 1 – simple sale ($100,000) – as the farmer you will not have anything more to do with the following transactions
- Trade 2 – simple sale ($100,000)
- Trade 3 – buyer worried he had overpaid on some bellies earlier in the year and wants to reduce the average price paid, buys contract ($100,000)
- Trade 4 – to a speculator who is aware that the price of next-season pork bellies is rising – the original contract has gone up in value, although the real bellies remain at $100,000.

So, there has been $400,000 dollars of notional action for the actual bellies. The market for the derivatives themselves, however, is far larger than for the goods. As always, the model depends on assumptions and everything goes well, until market conditions change.

The activity below puts students in the position of role-playing international trading. They might come up with alternative solutions to the current individualistic and national drives for growth that ignore environmental and ecological concerns.

The Trading Game

In December, 1993, a school near Bristol arranged a three-day programme of activities for students aged between 11 and 15 years focused on the theme world awareness. As part of this event, students played the 'Trading Game'. An article, headed *Pupils are learning about wider world*, was published on the Schools Page of the Chipping Sodbury Gazette, in which the trading game was described:

> The trade and aid theme was extended by the Mathematics department, who organised a simulation exercise based on a UNICEF idea for understanding the economic relationship between the developed and the developing world.

This description was followed by various people's experiences of the game:

> One of the organisers and the UN representative [in the game], said 'The simulation helps the children to become aware of the trading that goes on between countries in the real world. When one country has something that another needs, then they trade'. Another of the organisers, Ms L. Brown, added: 'They have done really well. The game introduced them to different uses of Maths as well as getting them involved in team work. They found that rich groups were not eager to trade with poor groups. This shows what happens in the real world.'

Students reported, 'It was brilliant. I'd like to have played it all day,' (Kelvin, aged 11) and Louise, another Year Seven student added: 'It was interesting because it showed how hard it is for poor countries to get what they need.'

In 1992, some criteria for assessing attitudes for Economic Understanding (National Curriculum Council (NCC) publication, *Mathematics and Economic and Industrial Understanding at Key Stages 3 and 4*, p. 4), were published for schools:

- an interest in economic and industrial affairs
- respect for evidence and rational argument in economic contexts
- concern for the use of scarce resources
- a sense of responsibility for the consequences of their own economic actions, as individuals and members of groups
- respect for alternative economic viewpoints and a willingness to reflect critically on their own economic views and values
- sensitivity to the effects of economic choices on the environment
- concern for human rights, as these are affected by economic decisions.

Given that these criteria were written in 1992, how would you change and develop them for the world now? They already support the reflective knowing from Chapter 1. Can you use them to assess your pupils using the following game?

The Trading Game, used in the World Awareness days at the school above, was a case study in the same NCC publication. Although this publication is out of print, how to play the trading game is described in detail on the Christian Aid website with the introduction:

> Current world trading systems are helping to maintain the gap between rich and poor nations. These are systems that help strong well-organised nations such as the USA and the EU states, rather than poorer countries. The Trading Game helps to show how trade affects the prosperity of a country – both positively and negatively. It is a fun and exciting introduction to the issues of trade, providing a simple outline of some very complex relationships. It is a valuable introduction to the basic issues that determine how the gap between rich and poor nations is maintained.

Starting point

Invite students to write down as many three-letter words as they can in a minute. Start timing immediately after you have finished giving the instruction and do not answer questions from those who want to know 'why' or fuss about finding a pencil. You want there to be a range of numbers of three-letter-word responses. The total number of words written by each student per minute is their output and will remain constant. Say the output ranges from 20 to five words, pick a number in the middle and say that they need to produce 12 words a minute to satisfy the bank. Let this run for a number of minutes and see what happens. Some students have a surplus and might do a deal with a student who cannot produce enough words. The problem of course is that the students with low output cannot get out of the ever-increasing debt cycle. This activity will set up the more complex scenario of the trading game.

Lesson plan (students aged 13–14 years)

The following notes are what are left from my final planning notes when I organised the game at a school in 1993 and can be supplemented by those on the Christian Aid website:

Time required: At least 1.5 hours, and preferably 2 hours including discussion afterwards. Two authority figures: the Banker and the United Nations representative who judges disputes and is able to offer support.

1. Eight groups of seven pupils, organised so that there are mixed tables between classes and of achievement of the pupils.
2. Each group will have different equipment, organise the tables with equipment on. Recommended ratios from the NCC publication are written below. (For 30 pupils the publication recommends six groups of five pupils in each with one group of type A, three of type B and two of type C.) You will, of course, need to adapt for the numbers of students in your game. Envelopes with resources in are placed on each table at the start.
   - *Group A* (1 group): 4 pencils; 2 rulers; 1 set square; 3 sheets of A4 paper; 5 cards worth £10,000 each; 2 semicircular protractors; 2 pairs of compasses; 2 pairs of scissors.
   - *Group B* (3 groups):
     - B1: 1 pencil; 1 pair of compasses; 2 cards worth £10,000 each; 1 protractor; 3 sheets of A4 paper.
     - B2: 1 pencil; 1 sheet of A4 paper; 2 cards worth £5000 each; 1 ruler; 1 set square.
     - B3: 1 pencil; 2 sheets of A4 paper; 2 cards worth £1000 each; 1 ruler; 1 pair of scissors.
   - *Group C* (2 groups):
     - C1: 1 pencil; 2 sheets of coloured A4 paper; 5 sheets of A4 paper.
     - C2: 1 ruler; 2 cards worth £500 each; 3 sheets of A4 paper.

3. Organise bank: Poster created to put on wall of the kinds of products (geometric shapes), which can be made and sold to the bank:
   - a rectangle 5cm × 7cm worth £200
   - an equilateral triangle of side 5cm worth £250
   - a semicircle, the same size as the protractor, worth £300
   - a circle of radius 10cm worth £500
   - a square of side 6cm worth £100
   - a right-angled triangle of sides 6, 8 and 10cm worth £150.

   We used green sugar paper and pink card for the geometric shapes with large felt pen writing in bold colours. The bank also had spares of scissors/paper etc that could be used during the game for loans to keep the game moving. The UN representative might give aid, for instance.

4. *Introduction*: This is World Development Day. Each table is a country and countries trade! The World Bank has announced a world shortage of these shapes and your task will be to make as much money as you can through working at making these shapes (pointing to poster). How to make them? There could well be more than one method. You have different sets of equipment.

5. The Bank buys the shapes but will only buy accurate shapes; for instance, edges *must* be cut by scissors! Only one person at any time can be at the Bank. Tables can trade just like countries do. At various times there might be a world glut or a world shortage of particular shapes with consequent changes to values of different shapes and these will be announced by the Banker or the UN representative. There might also be announced premiums for various colours of paper (equivalent to gold, silver being found). For more sophisticated mathematics, if things are going well, loans and interest could be introduced.

6. Leave time for discussion and reflection. What did it feel like in the various countries? What would you change if you played the game again? What is possible to change?

Ways forward

It is understandable if the less-developed world wants the resources and standards of living of the developed world. There is a 'de-growth' movement that argues for the downscaling and contraction of economies and those who argue this is not necessary (Ben-Ami 2009). However, we are not at the start of the industrial revolution in Europe, with seemingly limitless raw materials and a policy of 'grow first, clean up later' (*The Economist* 2012: 64). There are countless stories of profligate waste of the Earth's natural resources in the early days of industrialisation, even into the 1960s (e.g. 'The Cuyahoga river in Ohio was so polluted that it caught fire as recently as 1969', *The Economist* 2012: 64).

There do seem now to be examples where different awarenesses prevail and values and ecological considerations are built into business models that adapt to circumstances in the developing world. An example tells of one-fifth of the roses exported to Europe being grown in Kenya's Rift Valley, providing one-tenth of Kenya's foreign exchange. Attracted by the money, a quarter of a million people arrived. To live, they ploughed the surrounding hills, felling trees that filtered the streams flowing into the lake, which became polluted by silt and run-off. The story does not end there, though; the rose growers started to lend money to the smallholders, encouraging modern farming methods that leave the trees in place, benefiting growers, small farmers and the lake (*The Economist* 2012: 64). The environment could be seen as another kind of capital. An alternative view would be to cut consumption – why does Europe need all those roses? What else could be grown?

There are already examples of sustainable and green growth where the ecological footprint is considered. An ecological footprint is a measure of the maximum consumption or resource use that an area has the capacity to sustain, taking into consideration the need to assimilate waste products and regenerate. For example, the world footprint asks, do we fit on the planet?:

> Today humanity uses the equivalent of 1.5 planets to provide the resources we use and absorb our waste. This means it now takes the Earth one year and six months to regenerate what we use in a year. Moderate UN scenarios suggest that if current population and consumption trends continue, by the 2030s, we will need the equivalent of two Earths to support us. And of course, we only have one. Turning resources into waste faster than waste can be turned back into resources puts us in global ecological overshoot, depleting the very resources on which human life and biodiversity depend.
>
> (Global Footprint Network, online)

Previously growth has been seen to be infinite but now, with a shift in perspective, a limit has been proposed, that of the capacity of the Earth to sustain us. Of course, this still involves calculations but is important to contemplate if the following analogy is valid:

> Neoclassical economics, like classical physics, is relevant to a special case that assumes that we are far from limits – far from the limiting speed of light or the limiting smallness of an elementary particle in physics – and far from the biophysical limits of the earth's carrying capacity and ethico-social limits of satiety in economics. Just as in physics, so in economics: the classical theories do not work well in regions close to limits.
>
> (Daly 1996: 37)

If we are approaching the limits of the planet's capacity in terms of waste and extraction, then the models of growth we are used to will stop working. What does 'sustainable growth' look like? What do the green economists advocate for the post-growth world? We need to take responsibility for coming to a view on growth ourselves and support our students in doing the same. In the words of the author John Lanchester, we need to know 'how to make the finance industry back into something which serves the rest of society, rather than just predating on it' (Lanchester 2010: 232).

Further reading

- There is an excellent tutorial on supply/demand/equilibrium on the Investopedia site, http://www.investopedia.com/university/economics/economics3. asp#axzz2Lr6mnr00. This site also includes a searchable set of definitions and explanations of financial terms.
- There is a tutorial entitled *Black–Scholes versus Binomial* (http://www.youtube. com/watch?v=oTFHBKtDLw0, accessed 5 Aug 2012) on the web that has a running time of just under six minutes. You will also be led to other tutorials and background to the current crisis on a video called *The Money Masters* (http://www. youtube.com/watch?v=svly7TJMtzw, accessed 24 Feb 2013).
- The Christian Aid website (accessed 7 Aug 2012) is essential reading if you are going to play the trading game with students of any age: http://learn.christianaid. org.uk/YouthLeaderResources/trading_game.aspx and http://learn.christianaid. org.uk/Images/trading_game_intro_to_the_game_tcm16-28864.pdf. Do not be afraid to add constraints and support as they occur to you or change the commodities.

References

Attenborough, D. (2011) People and Planet, RSA President's Lecture. Available online at http://www.thersa.org/events/video/vision-videos/sir-david-attenborough (accessed 10 July 2012).

Banks, I. M. (1994) A Few Notes on the Culture. Available online at http://www.vavatch.co.uk/books/banks/cultnote.htm (accessed 4 February 2012).

Ben-Ami, D. (2009) *Ferraris for all: in defence of economic progress*. Bristol: The Policy Press.

Christian Aid (n.d.) The trading game. Available online at http://learn.christianaid.org.uk/YouthLeaderResources/trading_game.aspx (accessed 12 December 2011).

Daly, H. (1996) *Beyond growth: the economics of sustainable development,* Boston, MA: Beacon Press.

Dickinson, E. (2011) GDP: a brief history – one stat to rule them all, *Foreign Policy*, Jan/Feb. Available online at http://www.foreignpolicy.com/articles/2011/01/02/gdp_a_brief_history (accessed 6 June 2012).

The Economist (2012) Shoots, greens and leaves, green growth, 16–22 June: 64-66.

Global Footprint Network (2012) World footprint: do we fit on the planet? Available online at http://www.footprintnetwork.org/en/index.php/GFN/page/world_footprint/ (accessed 8 August 2012).

Granovetter, Mark (2005) The impact of social structure on economic outcomes. *Journal of Economic Perspectives* 19 (1): 33–50.

The Guardian (2009) UK GDP since 1955, 25 November. Available online at http://www. guardian.co.uk/news/datablog/2009/nov/25/gdp-uk-1948-growth-economy (accessed 20 October 2012).

Hern, W. M. (1999) How many times has the human population doubled? Comparisons with cancer. *Population and Environment: A Journal of Interdisciplinary Studies* 21(1): 59–80.

International Monetary Fund (IMF) (2012) World economic outlook, real GDP growth. Available online at http://www.imf.org/external/datamapper/index.php (accessed 8 August 2012).

Investopedia (n.d.) http://www.investopedia.com (accessed 24 Feb 2013).

Kunzig, R. (2011) Population 7 billion: how your world will change, Seven Billion Special Series, *National Geographic*, 42–49: 60–63.

Lanchester, J. (2010) *I.O.U.: why everyone owes everyone and no one can pay,* London: Simon and Schuster.

Meadows, D. H., Meadows, D. L., Randers, J. and Behrens, W. W. (1972) *The limits to growth,* New York: Potomac Associates.

Meadows, D. H., Randers, J. and Meadows, D. L., (2004), *Limits to growth: the 30-year update,* London: Earthscan.

Stewart, I. (2012) Is this the equation that caused the crash?, *The Observer,* 12 February: 18.

Summers, D. (2008) No return to boom and bust: what Brown said when he was chancellor, *The Guardian,* 11 September. Available online at http://www.guardian.co.uk/politics/2008/sep/11/gordonbrown.economy (accessed 7 August 2012).

Climate change

Richard Barwell

The Intergovernmental Panel on Climate Change (IPCC), the UN-organised body that reviews scientific research on climate change, concluded in its most recent assessment that 'Warming of the climate system is unequivocal' (IPCC 2008: 72). The NASA website states 'The evidence for climate change is compelling' (NASA 2012). The UK's Met Office (2009) recently stated, 'It is now clear that man-made greenhouse gases are causing climate change. The rate of change began as significant, has become alarming and is simply unsustainable in the long term' (p. 2).

These quotes highlight two things. First, that there is a widespread scientific consensus that climate change is caused by human activity and is a major threat. Second, that there is a huge amount of information about climate change available to anyone with an internet connection. Climate change is now the frequent topic of reports in newspapers, in broadcast media, on blogs and websites. Al Gore's film *An Inconvenient Truth*, which shows Gore travelling around North America giving a presentation on climate change, even won an Oscar. In all these diverse sources of information and opinion, mathematics is a constant, if often unremarked, presence. This observation leads to several questions:

- What mathematics is involved in understanding climate change?
- How is mathematics used or misused in arguments and debates about the need for action?
- What mathematics do 'consumers' of information about climate change need to know to be able to make informed judgments about what they are reading?
- How do the interests of authors of information about climate change influence their use of mathematics?

One of the purposes of this chapter is to make visible the role of mathematics in understanding and reporting climate change. More than this, however, the chapter will examine how mathematics in some sense makes climate change real. Without mathematics, it would be difficult to have a global view of climate change. Mathematics is, therefore, crucial to our understanding of climate change. At the same time, mathematics, including the mathematics embedded in technology, is implicated in causing climate change and in what we understand climate change to be. Finally, as argued in Chapter 1, issues like climate change are not just scientifically complex, they are socially complex. As such, any response to climate change must be developed with the participation of all of us – not just as teachers, but as citizens – since it will potentially involve significant changes to how we live (see Hulme 2009). And to participate, we all need to understand some of the mathematics of climate change and, in particular, so will our students. So, as well as exploring some of the mathematics of climate change, this chapter suggests some ways in which this mathematics could be used in the classroom.

Climate change and mathematics

First, an important distinction: *weather* refers to the meteorological conditions at a specific time and place. Look outside and note the temperature, wind conditions, cloud cover, precipitation and so on – that is the weather where you are. *Climate* is simply statistics: the statistics of weather. For example, to say that the climate of Scotland is cooler than that of England is to make a statistical statement. More precisely, the statement means that the mean temperature of Scotland over a given, reasonably long period of time is lower than the mean temperature of England over the same period. On specific days, however, the temperature may be much higher or lower than the long-term mean and the temperature in Scotland may be higher than the temperature in England (see Table 3.1 for an example).

This definition of climate as the statistics of weather can be extended to climate *change*. Here is a definition of climate change proposed by the IPCC in their most recent report:

> a change in the state of the climate that can be identified (e.g. using statistical tests) by changes in the mean and/or the variability of its properties, and that persists for an extended period, typically decades or longer.

(IPCC 2008: 30)

Climate change is thus described in terms of changes in means as identified by statistical tests. These techniques are applied to a wide variety of data, including air and sea temperature recordings and other standard meteorological readings, as well as records of such things as glacial melting or sea level (both are increasing: see IPCC 2008: 30). It is worth noting that much of this mathematics is well within the scope of school mathematics curricula.

In Chapter 1, I discussed the mathematics of description, prediction and communication. The description of climate change, then, makes great use of (often

Table 3.1 Comparing the climate and weather of Edinburgh and London

	Climate	**Weather**
	Mean daily maximum temperature (°C) 1971–2000	Maximum temperature (°C) 25 October 2011
Edinburgh	12.2	9.5
London (Greenwich)	14.8	16.8

Source: http://www.metoffice.gov.uk/climate/uk/averages/19712000/ and http://weather.lgfl.org.uk/Default.aspx

basic) statistics, both to establish long-term average conditions, as well as to examine climate variability. The mean daily maximum temperature in Edinburgh only tells us part of the story of Edinburgh's climate: it is also useful to know how much the daily maximum varies from this mean and how frequently. How often will Edinburgh experience sub-zero temperatures, for example? Or extreme heat? In addition to the statistical description of the climate, similar mathematics is involved in assessing greenhouse gas emissions, as well as the wider impact of climate change on our society.

The prediction of climate change uses more advanced mathematics. Developing predictions about future global, regional or local effects of climate change draw on a range of advanced mathematics, including mathematical modelling, differential equations, non-linear systems and stochastic processes (McKenzie 2007: 22–3). Several different climate models have been developed to relate greenhouse gas emissions to changes in the Earth's climate. Various mathematical techniques are used to validate these models, such as testing them on historical data.

The communication of climate change also involves mathematics. Climate change is now explained or discussed in a wide range of non-scientific contexts, including the mass media, official websites, blogs, official publications, reports and so on. Interpreting and, in some cases, participating in the production of these texts entails some level of engagement with the mathematics used to describe and predict climate change. Additionally, a degree of 'mathematical literacy' is also necessary, in relation to the use and interpretation of data, graphs and accounts of the mathematics involved. Newspaper articles, for example, now regularly include graphs or other mathematical graphics showing global temperature changes, emissions data and so on. Moreover, there are several examples of public debate in which mathematical considerations have been significant. Such considerations include arguments about the misrepresentation of data, about the status of predictions made on the basis of mathematical climate models and discussion about the concept of a long-term trend (in the light of particularly cold winter weather, for example). Policy makers, public servants, business and the general public are all, increasingly, consumers of information (and, in some cases, polemic) about climate change. The central role of mathematics in climate science, along with the increasing political and public attention that climate change is attracting, suggests an important role for education in general and mathematics education in particular.

Critical mathematics education and climate change

Without information technology, our understanding of climate change would be severely limited. Even the basic mathematical processes involved in calculating long-term norms or trends would be time-consuming and unwieldy when faced with the huge quantities of time-series data generated by multiple weather stations on multiple occasions. And without mathematical modelling and the mathematics of differential equations, non-linear systems, stochastic processes and so on, scenarios for the future of the climate of the planet, such as those presented by the IPCC (2008), would be more or less impossible to produce. Climate models, for example, typically include over a million lines of computer code and need to run for many days to generate modelling data representing a few decades of global climate (Weaver 2008).

The projections derived from these models are, however, already more than abstract scientific theories. They are having tangible social effects, from discussion and debate, to changing individual and organisational behaviour, to the creation of new national and international structures (see DEFRA 2009 for some examples). The description and prediction of climate change are thus good examples of the formatting power of mathematics: through mathematisation, social reality is changed. In this case, however, mathematical communication is a particularly important channel for this power. The formatting power of the mathematics of climate change arises somewhat differently from the formatting power of the airline ticket sales model (Skovsmose 2001, see Chapter 1), in which the model is embedded within the technology and the technology is then embedded within social practice. In the case of climate change, the mathematics is embedded in technology used by scientists, not by the general public. The outcomes of scientists' work are then transformed, through communication, to appear within a range of different discourses (political, governmental, mass media). It is these mathematical communications that are then embedded within social practice.

The mathematics of climate change involves all three of Skovsmose's forms of knowing (again, see Chapter 1). Mathematical knowing concerns the mathematics involved in describing or predicting climate change, as well as in communicating climate change, as summarised earlier in this paper. Technological knowing involves knowing how to construct the mathematical tools necessary for understanding climate change. In describing climate change, for instance, the calculation of global temperature increases involves some specific ways of using recorded temperatures and arithmetic means (see Example 1: What is normal?). Technological knowing also involves knowing how to use these tools, such as how to interpret the resulting means. Given the central role of mathematics in the communication of climate change, we can also include technological knowing relating to the construction and interpretation of graphical or linguistic representations of climate changes or the related mathematical processes. Being able to make sense of a graph showing three possible future climate scenarios (related to three different emissions scenarios) is as much a part of technological knowing as being able to construct the models that lead to these projections.

Reflective knowing about the mathematics of climate change potentially involves an awareness of several different issues. These issues include the following points.

- An awareness of the effects of the various decisions made in the mathematisation of climate processes, such as what is included or excluded from a model. Given some of the (sometimes bizarre) debates that are taking place, it is important that mathematical modelling, for example, is understood as a general process.
- An awareness of the formatting power of mathematics in relation to climate change. As argued above, this power is derived from communication processes. Critical citizens need to be able to interpret and participate in discussion and debate about climate change; they also need an awareness of how particular mathematical representations of climate change may be linked to the (potentially political) interests of the author.
- An awareness of the nature of the relationship between mathematics and science. While scientists generate data and physical models of the climate and the planetary ecosystem more broadly, their understanding of the specific nature of human-induced climate change is almost entirely due to mathematics.
- An awareness of human impacts on the climate. As Skovsmose recognises (1994: 170–4), mathematics provides a powerful way for learners and citizens to interpret and participate in society. In the context of climate change, mathematics provides a means to examine, for example, current emissions by country, by activity, or by individuals. In all three areas, wide disparities and inequities exist.

In the rest of this chapter, some of these ideas are illustrated through three examples. In the first example, which focuses on the mathematics of describing climate change, I look at how long-term climate statistics are calculated. The second example looks at some aspects relating to the predicted frequency of extreme weather events in a warming global climate. In the third example, which focuses on communicating climate change, I examine data on greenhouse gas emissions to consider how different ways of representing data can tell different kinds of story.

Example 1: What is normal?

Climate change is increasingly in the news. Look at the selection of headlines and extracts below. What mathematics is involved?

Flood warnings: hottest year confirms global warming say experts

The two most respected national weather services in the US, NASA and the National Oceanic and Atmospheric Administration (NOAA), agreed that 2010 tied with 2005 as the hottest since records began in 1880.

Overall 2010 and 2005 were 1.12°F (0.62°C) above the 20th century average when taking a combination of land and water surface temperatures across the world.

(*Daily Telegraph*, 13 January 2011)

Met Office: 2010 was second warmest year on record

Last year was the second warmest on record after 1998, the Met Office announced today. With a mean temperature of 14.5°C, 2010 was 0.5°C warmer than the global average from 1961–1990, according to data from the Met Office and the University of East Anglia.

The UK recorded its coldest year since 1986 and its coldest December in 100 years, according to the Met Office. However, very few parts of the world were significantly colder than normal during 2010.

(*The Guardian*, 20 January 2011)

Forget the chill, 2010 was India's hottest year on record
NEW DELHI: Severe cold may well be making headlines in the past two weeks, but here's the big picture: 2010 was the warmest year ever in India since weather records began in 1901. The Indian Meteorological Department announced on Thursday that the mean annual temperature in the country during 2010 was as much as 0.93 degrees Celsius higher than the long term (1961–1990) average.

IMD officials said the record heat in 2010 was a continuation of the warming trend in the past decade that can only be attributed to global warming. The last decade has been the warmest in the country's history. The previous warmest year was 2009, when the annual mean temperature was 0.913 degrees C above the long term average.

(*Times of India*, 14 January 2011)

How do you take the temperature of a planet? It turns out, perhaps not surprisingly, that you do not. The above reports are based on analysis of millions of temperature records from weather stations around the world. While the quantity of data is mind-boggling, much of the mathematics is fairly straightforward. There are two key concepts that underlie most of the calculations.

Long-term averages refer to the arithmetic mean of climate data (e.g. temperature, precipitation, hours of sunshine) over a given period of time. The World Meteorological Organisation stipulates the use of 30-year periods, although sometimes 100-year periods are also used. Thirty years is considered to be the minimum period necessary to eliminate the effects of year-to-year variation. In the UK, these long-term averages are updated every decade (see Met Office n.d.). For example, the long-term monthly average minimum and maximum temperatures for Sheffield for the period 1971–2000 are shown in Table 3.2.

Anomaly refers to the difference between a given data point and a long-term average. So, for example, a recorded maximum temperature in Sheffield on 3 October 2011 of 24.7°C represents an anomaly of 11.4°C with respect to the long-term October average. Anomalies can also be calculated for means: the mean maximum temperature for October 2011 can be compared with the long-term average mean. The anomaly is simply the difference between them. Table 3.3 shows temperature anomalies in annual means in Sheffield for the period 1981–2010.

Anomalies can be averaged across multiple locations, providing they all relate to the same 30-year period. The advantage of working with anomalies rather than actual temperatures is that they eliminate the effects of local geography. A weather station in the mountains will record cooler temperatures than a weather station in the lowlands, even if they are quite close together (e.g. at the top of Snowdon *vs.* in Bangor on

Table 3.2 Average minimum and maximum temperatures for Sheffield for the period 1971–2000

	Max Temp (°C)	Min Temp (°C)
January	6.4	1.6
February	6.7	1.6
March	9.3	3.1
April	11.8	4.4
May	15.7	7.0
June	18.3	10.0
July	20.8	12.4
August	20.6	12.1
September	17.3	10.0
October	13.3	7.2
November	9.2	4.2
December	7.2	2.6
Year	13.1	6.4

Data source: http://www.metoffice.gov.uk/climate/uk/averages/19712000/sites/sheffield.html

the coast). By calculating a long-term average for each location and then calculating anomalies in relation to that long-term average, we might see, for example, that each location has recorded temperatures 1°C above the long-term average, even if the actual temperatures were different.

The 30-year long-term average, then, is the standard definition of 'normal'. In a stable climate, we might expect any 30-year period to produce similar norms, with even less variation apparent when considering 100-year norms. And in a stable climate, we might also expect the anomalies to be fairly evenly distributed around the long-term averages. In the case of temperature, for example, some years are hotter, some years are cooler, but over the long-term, the hotter and cooler years balance out.

A quick glance at the anomalies columns in Table 3.3, however, is enough to see that there are more negative anomalies in the top half of the table compared with the bottom half. Representing the anomalies in graph form bears this out (see Figures 3.1 and 3.2). The graphs also include linear regression lines. The equations for these regression lines suggest that over the 30-year period, there is a mean increase in the annual mean temperature in Sheffield of 0.03°C per year, with an overall increase of a little under 1°C. An alternative representation of the long-term trend is also provided: the dotted lines represent five-year averages, which smooth out annual fluctuations. This line also shows a general increasing trend, although with a dip in the last part of the graph. Which of the two trend lines is more realistic? Does the linear regression line 'hide' a more recent cooling? How reasonable is it to construct a linear regression, given that the climate is a non-linear system? It is perhaps worth pointing out that the recent dip is still entirely above the long-term mean.

Table 3.3 Annual mean daily maximum and minimum temperature anomalies for Sheffield, UK, 1981–2010, relative to 1981–2010 norms.

	Maximum temperatures (°C)			Minimum temperatures (°C)		
	Annual mean max temp	Long-term average annual max temp (1981–2010)	Anomaly	Annual mean min temp	Long-term average annual min temp (1981–2010)	Anomaly
1981	12.5	13.4	−0.9	6.8	6.6	0.2
1982	13.5	13.4	0.1	6.4	6.6	−0.2
1983	13.2	13.4	−0.2	6.7	6.6	0.1
1984	13.3	13.4	−0.1	6.2	6.6	−0.4
1985	12.3	13.4	−1.1	5.8	6.6	−0.8
1986	12.1	13.4	−1.3	5.3	6.6	−1.3
1987	12.4	13.4	−1.0	5.8	6.6	−0.8
1988	13.1	13.4	−0.3	6.5	6.6	−0.1
1989	14.2	13.4	0.8	6.9	6.6	0.3
1990	14.3	13.4	0.9	7.3	6.6	0.7
1991	13.0	13.4	−0.4	6.3	6.6	−0.3
1992	13.3	13.4	−0.1	6.4	6.6	−0.2
1993	12.6	13.4	−0.8	5.9	6.6	−0.7
1994	13.3	13.4	−0.1	6.5	6.6	−0.1
1995	14.0	13.4	0.6	6.8	6.6	0.2
1996	12.4	13.4	−1	5.8	6.6	−0.8
1997	14.0	13.4	0.6	7.0	6.6	0.4
1998	13.5	13.4	0.1	7.0	6.6	0.4
1999	14.1	13.4	0.7	7.2	6.6	0.6
2000	13.5	13.4	0.1	6.9	6.6	0.3
2001	13.3	13.4	−0.1	6.4	6.6	−0.2
2002	13.9	13.4	0.5	7.2	6.6	0.6
2003	14.4	13.4	1	6.7	6.6	0.1
2004	13.9	13.4	0.5	7.5	6.6	0.9
2005	13.9	13.4	0.5	7.2	6.6	0.6
2006	14.2	13.4	0.8	7.4	6.6	0.8
2007	13.8	13.4	0.4	7.2	6.6	0.6
2008	13.4	13.4	0	6.9	6.6	0.3
2009	13.6	13.4	0.2	7.1	6.6	0.5
2010	12.4	13.4	−1	5.9	6.6	−0.7

Data source: http://www.metoffice.gov.uk/pub/data/weather/uk/climate/stationdata/sheffielddata.txt

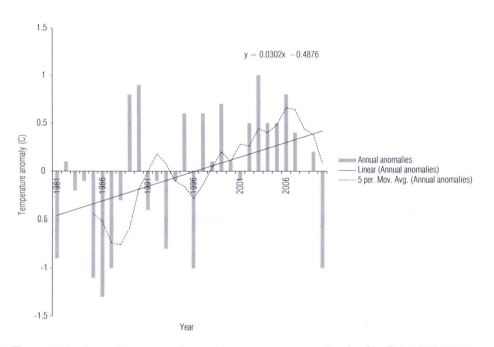

Figure 3.1   Annual mean maximum temperature anomalies for Sheffield, UK (1981–2010 baseline) (Based on data sourced from http://www.metoffice.gov.uk/pub/data/weather/uk/climate/stationdata/sheffielddata.txt /)

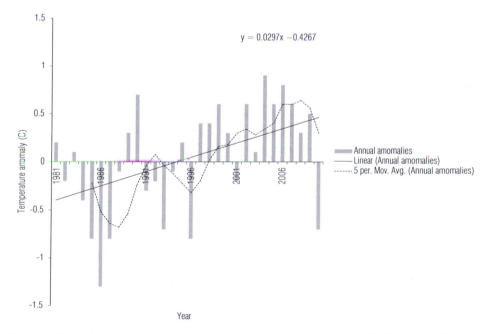

Figure 3.2   Annual mean minimum temperature anomalies for Sheffield, UK (1981–2010 baseline) (Based on data sourced from http://www.metoffice.gov.uk/pub/data/weather/uk/climate/stationdata/sheffielddata.txt /)

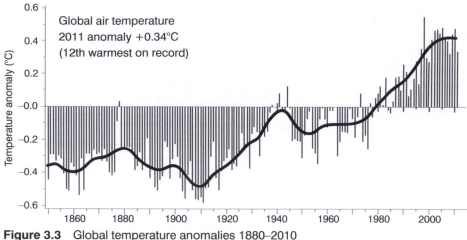

Figure 3.3 Global temperature anomalies 1880–2010
Source: Jones (2011) see http://www.cru.uea.ac.uk/cru/info/warming © Copyright 2012, Climatic Research Unit.

Furthermore, the long-term norms for 1971–2000 are below those for 1981–2010. Indeed, a similar graph for global data for the whole of the last century looks very similar to the graphs for Sheffield (see Figure 3.3). This data is based on averaging temperature anomalies across the globe.

These graphs suggest that both locally and globally, temperatures are steadily rising. The purpose of the preceding account is not particularly to persuade you that our planet is warming, although it might do this. Its purpose is more to give some sense of how meteorological data is, and can be, collated and examined to find out about long-term trends.

In terms of mathematics teaching, there are a couple of points of interest. First, with the exception of linear regression, all the preceding information is based on arithmetic means and basic arithmetic. Second, meteorological data for many locations in the UK are available online. And there is something powerful and immediate about analysing data for where *you* live. The information about temperatures in Sheffield was obtained from the Met Office website which provides monthly mean maximum and minimum temperatures. Using a spreadsheet, annual means, long-term means and anomalies were calculated. The graphs and trendlines were also prepared using a spreadsheet.

The above methods raise many questions that could form starting points for classroom investigation. What happens if different long-term norms are calculated? e.g. 10-years? 20-years? 50-years? What happens to running averages, as shown in Figures 3.1 and 3.2, if different periods are used? e.g. 2-year, 5-year or 10-year? What trends are apparent in other meteorological data? e.g. rainfall? How do these trends relate to the trends in temperature? These kinds of questions are about both mathematics and climate change. Exploring them should lead to a better understanding of both. An understanding of the mathematics of temperature trends will better equip students to participate in the associated debates about the nature of climate change and about the kind of action that might be necessary to respond to it.

Example 2: If the planet is warming, why was the winter of 2010–2011 so cold?

Hardly a snowfall goes by in the UK without opinion pieces appearing in the newspapers telling us that there is no climate change. The winter of 2010–2011 was the coldest for several years and there were suggestions that it indicated the start of a cooling trend. In fact, there are good mathematical reasons to expect some extreme cold weather events as a result of global warming (as others have already argued: see Weaver 2008, and Whiteley 2011).

Consider the range of temperatures experienced where you live. Some days are warmer, some are cooler, some are about average. The varying temperatures can be thought of as distributed around the long-term average. Extreme heat or extreme cold occur much more rarely than temperatures close to the long-term average. In fact this kind of pattern is apparent in the data shown for Sheffield. Most of the anomalies are clustered close to 0, with only a few extremes standing out in the graphs shown in Figures 3.1 and 3.2.

If the climate is warming, however, as we have seen, the long-term average will itself shift to a higher value. Perhaps in 30 years' time, the long-term average in Sheffield will be another 1°C above its current value. What would this mean for the distribution of temperatures from day to day or week to week? A starting assumption would be that the whole distribution as currently experienced would simply shift 1°C further up. This assumption is illustrated in Figure 3.4(a), which shows a 'current' distribution of temperatures and a 'future' distribution shifted along the x-axis. The figure also shows that in this scenario, we would expect to experience more extreme heat events and no extreme cold. This scenario corresponds to many people's expectations of the effects of climate change.

The climate is, however, not that simple (in mathematical terms, it is non-linear). In particular, an increase in global temperature means that there is more energy in the atmosphere. More energy results in greater variability, whether in terms of wind, precipitation or temperature. Consider, for a moment, what would happen if our starting distribution (e.g. of temperatures in Sheffield) was affected by an increase in variance, but not of temperature. As the total number of readings is fixed, the effect would be to flatten the distribution, spreading it out at the ends. In other words, there would be an increase in frequency of weather at the extremes, both hot and cold. This scenario is illustrated in Figure 3.4(b).

Increasing temperature will result in increased variance, however, so the two preceding scenarios need to be combined. Our initial distribution will shift along the x-axis, but the distribution will also flatten as variance increases. This scenario is illustrated in Figure 3.4(c). Depending on the x-axis shift, the resulting scenario could conceivably include a slightly greater number of extreme cold events, in addition to an increase in the number of extreme heat events. The combination shown in Figure 3.4(c) implies a similar frequency of extreme cold events, and a large increase in hot and extreme heat events. Hence it is entirely expectable that global warming will still involve unusually cold weather from time to time. Of course this scenario does not make it possible to predict precisely when extreme hot

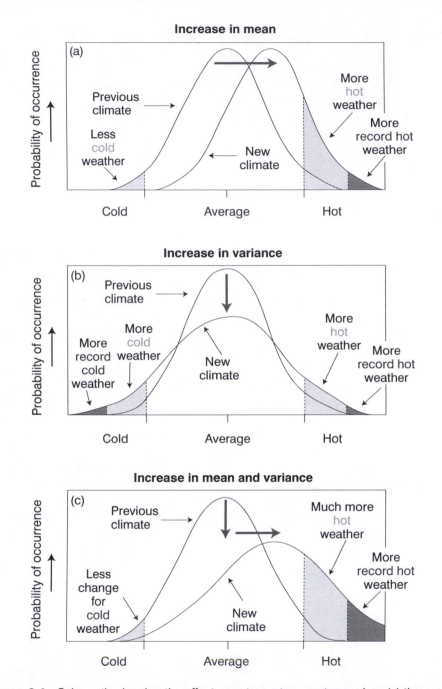

Figure 3.4 Schematic showing the effect on extreme temperatures when (a) the mean temperature increases, (b) the variance increases, and (c) when both the mean and variance increase for a normal distribution of temperature.

Source: *Climate change 2001: the scientific basis*. Contribution of Working Group I to the Third assessment report of the Intergovernmental Panel on Climate Change, Figure 2.32. Cambridge: Cambridge University Press

Table 3.4 Mean maximum and minimum temperatures and standard deviations for two 30-year periods in Sheffield, UK

	Mean maximum temperature (°C)	Standard deviation (°C)	Mean minimum temperature (°C)	Standard deviation (°C)
1901–1930	12.6	0.51	6.0	0.39
1981–2010	13.4	0.66	6.6	0.56

Data source: http://www.metoffice.gov.uk/pub/data/weather/uk/climate/stationdata/sheffielddata.txt

or cold events might occur; it just gives information about the likely frequency of such events.

The argument above is a theoretical one, based on mathematical reasoning (about distributions) and physics (the effects of adding energy to the climate system). The argument can easily be tested. The Met Office data for Sheffield go back to the nineteenth century. Table 3.4 shows the long-term mean maximum and minimum temperatures and associated standard deviations for two thirty-year periods: 1901–1930 and 1981–2010.[1]

These calculations fit with the argument made above. Not only has the mean temperature increased in Sheffield, so has the variation in temperature, as indicated by the standard deviation. If annual mean temperatures are normally distributed around the long-term mean, we would expect 67 per cent of annual mean temperatures to be within one standard deviation of the long-term mean. And we would expect 95 per cent of annual mean temperatures to be within two standard deviations of the long-term mean. Extremely warm or cool years could be defined as the 5 per cent of years that fall outside of two standard deviations. These distributions are interpreted in Tables 3.5a and 3.5b.

The annual mean minimum temperature records fit closely the projection made above: over the past century, while the annual mean minimum temperature in Sheffield has increased by 0.6°C, the point representing two standard deviations below the mean has hardly changed. This means that the frequency of unusually cool years has not significantly changed, even though the majority of years have higher mean minimum temperatures than before. At the other end of the scale, the likelihood of years with much higher mean minimum temperatures has become much greater.

The calculations for annual mean maximum temperatures suggest that there has been a greater shift in mean maximum temperatures with less flattening of the distribution. Nevertheless, years in which the mean maximum temperature is below 12.0°C have not disappeared, but they have become much less likely, down from 15 per cent of years in 1901–1930 to 2.2 per cent of years in 1981–2010.

There are a couple of points to highlight here with respect to teaching mathematics. As with the previous example, the data used in this example are available online and the calculations were made using a spreadsheet. The mathematics involved is more advanced than the calculation of long-term averages, involving consideration of frequency distributions, variation and the calculation and meaning of standard

Table 3.5a Mean maximum temperature distributions for two 30-year periods in Sheffield, UK

	−2 standard deviations	−1 standard deviation	Mean maximum temperature (°C)	+1 standard deviation	+2 standard deviations
1901–1930	11.5	12.0	12.6	13.1	13.6
1981–2010	12.1	12.7	13.4	14.0	14.7

Data source: http://www.metoffice.gov.uk/pub/data/weather/uk/climate/stationdata/sheffielddata.txt

Table 3.5b Mean minimum temperature distributions for two 30-year periods in Sheffield, UK

	−2 standard deviations	−1 standard deviation	Mean minimum temperature (°C)	+1 standard deviation	+2 standard deviations
1901–1930	5.3	5.6	6.0	6.4	6.8
1981–2010	5.4	6.0	6.6	7.2	7.7

Data source: http://www.metoffice.gov.uk/pub/data/weather/uk/climate/stationdata/sheffielddata.txt

deviation. The mathematics has several points of mathematical interest, which could form useful starting points for students' work. For example, what happens to distributions of temperature data over time? Or over longer long-term periods? What happens to other meteorological data, such as precipitation or wind speed? What counts as 'extreme'? How frequently have extreme weather events been recorded? How have these frequencies changed over time? Again, these kinds of questions are about both mathematics and climate change. An understanding of the mathematics can enable students to critically evaluate newspaper reports of the end of climate change and to contribute to the associated debates.

Example 3: Who is to blame?

One of the major sticking points in international negotiations for action to minimise climate change comes down to an issue of fairness. Rich industrialised countries have become rich through burning fossil fuels to power their economies. Now that the effects on the climate have become apparent, the goal is to reduce fossil fuel emissions across the globe. Poorer countries and countries with emerging economies have argued that they cannot allow reductions in carbon emissions to stop the process of industrialisation, through which they hope to make life better for their citizens. They argue that since it is the industrialised nations that have polluted the atmosphere for well over a century, it is the industrialised nations that should carry the greater burden. In this section, I look at different ways of presenting emissions data to explore this issue. I focus on two nation-states: the UK and India. As with Example 1, the data

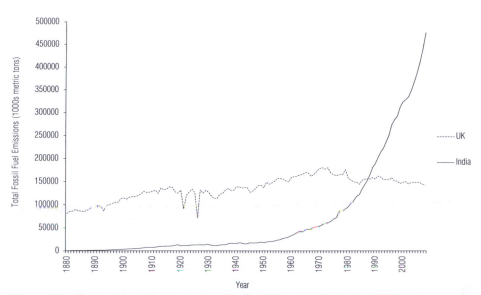

Figure 3.5   Annual fossil fuel emissions for the UK and India (1880–2008) (data source: http://cdiac.ornl.gov/ftp/ndp030/nation.1751_2008.ems)

used to produce the graphs are available online (at cdiac.ornl.gov) and the graphs were constructed using a spreadsheet.

First, look at Figure 3.5, which shows annual fossil fuel emissions for the two countries. This graph tells an interesting story. The UK's emissions have been relatively stable, approximately doubling over a period of 100 years, and declining slightly in the past 30 years. This decline may be attributed to a reduction in manufacturing in the UK, as well as to a shift from coal-fired to gas-fuelled power stations. In India, by contrast, emissions have increased sharply in an approximately exponential fashion. This sharp increase may be attributed to a growing level of industrialisation and consumption, combined with a rapidly increasing population. The graph also suggests that India is now a much bigger source of greenhouse gases than the UK (India is the third biggest emitter in the world). Now look at Figure 3.6, which shows *cumulative* emissions, based on the same data over the same period.

This graph presents things in a rather different light. The UK's relatively constant output over more than a century adds up to a vast quantity of greenhouse gas emissions. Carbon dioxide, the main greenhouse gas, remains in the atmosphere for at least a century, so that UK emissions from the first half of the twentieth century are still affecting the global climate now. India's emissions, by contrast, while now at a much higher annual rate than the UK's, are still cumulatively less. If current trends continue, however, India's cumulative emissions should overtake those of the UK in a fairly short time. So soon India will be a bigger polluter than the UK both annually *and* cumulatively – and it could therefore be argued that India is more 'to blame'. But what happens when we take into account the populations of the two countries? Look at Figure 3.7.

This graph shows a different picture again: while the UK's emissions per capita have fallen over the past decades, they remain five times higher than India's. Each

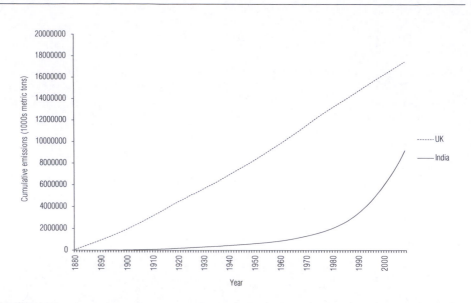

Figure 3.6 Cumulative fossil fuel emissions for the UK and India (1880–2008) (data source: http://cdiac.ornl.gov/ftp/ndp030/nation.1751_2008.ems)

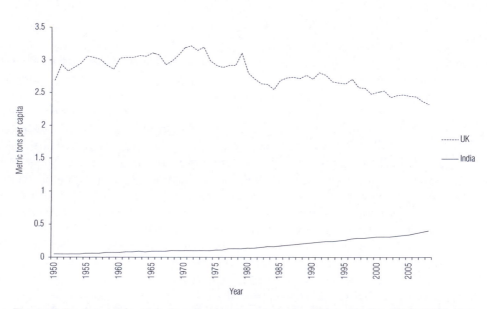

Figure 3.7 Annual fossil fuel emissions per capita for UK and India, 1950–2008 (data source: http://cdiac.ornl.gov/ftp/ndp030/nation.1751_2008.ems)

person in the UK produces on average five times more emissions than each person in India. On the other hand, India's per capita emissions have approximately quadrupled in the past 60 years. What might the future bring? UK per capita emissions seem to be declining somewhat, although they remain much higher than India's. In India, by contrast, the trend seems to be upward. It seems likely that if Indian consumption reaches industrialised levels, the per capita emissions will increase quite dramatically, with potentially disastrous effects on our planet.

I have presented just three representations of greenhouse gas emissions. Others could be considered. In particular, emissions data does not generally take into account 'offshore' emissions. Much of the emissions from China, for example, arise from manufacturing goods for export to North America and Europe. If these emissions are tallied under the totals for the country of consumption, greater differences are apparent. Recent analysis by Davis, Peters and Caldeira (2011) suggests that around 40 per cent of the emissions relating to the goods and services in the UK economy are produced overseas.

As with the previous examples, the above discussion suggests several starting points for mathematical investigation. These different graphs, for example, are based on the same data. Which gives a 'truer' picture? Perhaps the truest picture comes from looking at all of them. Nevertheless, consideration of the differences between the three graphs shows how they highlight different things. Now imagine you represent India in international climate negotiations: which graph would you present to support your case? What about if you represented the UK? Graphs are not entirely neutral. Part of a critical mathematics education is about learning to interrogate not only the data, but also the way it is represented, and to consider whose interests might be served by the particular choices that have been made.

Conclusions and future directions

Climate change is an issue of global concern that is increasingly likely to affect our lives in the coming century. Future citizens need a critical understanding of the role of mathematics in understanding climate change and a critical awareness of the ways that mathematics is communicated if they are to participate in the development of a global societal response. Mathematics education has a role to play in developing this critical awareness (Barwell 2013). Climate change is not an issue that we can simply leave to scientists to solve and tell the rest of us what measures we need to take to make the problem go away. The climate is a planetary-scale system, in which humans are one part of the biosphere. Interventions or actions to try to stop climate change or mitigate its effects cannot be introduced in isolation. For example, some governments have started to implement carbon taxes on air travel. But air travel is by its nature international, so this taxation has effects on the airline market. Or, to take another example, a decision to close coal-fired power stations would have a much greater impact on some countries than others. China's recent growth and the associated rise in living standards for many Chinese has been accompanied by a huge programme of power station construction. Thus the nature of climate change means that we all need to be involved in tackling the problem, not just in changing our behaviour, but in participating in the discussion and debate about what to do (Hulme 2009). And participating in this discussion requires a degree of mathematical understanding. The purpose of this chapter has been to show a little of the nature of this mathematics and show how it relates to an understanding of some aspects of climate change. As mathematics teachers, we have an important role to play in educating our students to participate in the debate.

Further reading

■ The London Grid for Learning Weather Monitoring System includes detailed historical weather data as well as real-time records for many locations around the UK: http://weather.lgfl.org.uk/Default.aspx (accessed 19 July 2012).

■ Met Office Climate Averages – 1971–2000 averages for several different climate variables for many locations around the UK: http://www.metoffice.gov.uk/climate/uk/averages/ (accessed 19 July 2012).

■ The American Mathematical Society's Mathematics Awareness Month for 2009 was on 'Mathematics and Climate'. It consists of a set of short essays and podcasts on a variety of topics related to this theme, all available online: http://www.mathaware.org/mam/09/essays.html (accessed 19 July 2012).

Note

1 The data for Sheffield consist of monthly mean minimum and maximum temperatures. The record for 1901–1930 is incomplete: the data for some months are missing in 1918, 1919 and 1923. These entire years were therefore not included in calculations of means and standard deviations. The standard deviations were calculated using a spreadsheet.

References

Barwell, R. (2013) The mathematical formatting of climate change: critical mathematics education and post-normal science. *Research in Mathematics Education* 15(1) 1–16.

Davis, S. J., Peters, G. P. and Caldeira, K. (2011) The supply chain of CO_2 emissions, *PNAS* 108 (45) 18554–9.

Department for Environment, Food and Rural Affairs (UK) (DEFRA) (2009) *Adapting to climate change: UK climate projections*, London: DEFRA.

The Guardian (2011) Met Office: 2010 was second warmest year on record. January 20. Available online at http://www.guardian.co.uk/environment/2011/jan/20/met-office-2010-second-warmest-year (accessed 20 March 2013).

Hulme, M. (2009) *Why we disagree about climate change: understanding controversy, inaction and opportunity*, Cambridge, Cambridge University Press.

Jones, P. (2011) Global temperature record. Climate Research Unit, University of East Anglia Available online at http://www.cru.uea.ac.uk/cru/info/warming/ (accessed 8 August 2012).

Intergovernmental Panel on Climate Change (IPCC) (2008) *Climate change 2007 synthesis report*, Geneva: IPCC.

McKenzie, D. (2007) *Mathematics of climate change: a new discipline for an uncertain century*, Berkeley, CA.: Mathematical Sciences Research Institute.

Met Office (2009) *Warming: climate change – the facts*, Exeter: The Met Office.

Met Office (n.d.) Climate averages. Available online at http://www.metoffice.gov.uk/climate/uk/averages/ (accessed 20 March 2013).

NASA (2012) Global climate change. Available online at http://climate.nasa.gov/evidence/ (accessed 6 August 2012).

Skovsmose, O. (1994) *Towards a philosophy of critical mathematics education,* Dordrecht: Kluwer.

Skovsmose, O. (2001) Mathematics in action: a challenge for social theorising. In E. Simmt, and B. Davis (eds) *Proceedings of the 2001 annual meeting of the Canadian Mathematics Education Study Group*. Edmonton, AB: CMESG.

The Telegraph (2011) Flood warnings: hottest year confirms global warming say experts. Available online at http://www.telegraph.co.uk/earth/earthnews/8257317/Flood-warnings-hottest-year-confirms-global-warming-say-experts.html (accessed 20 March 2013).

The Times of India (2011) Forget the chill, 2010 was India's hottest year on record. http://articles.timesofindia.indiatimes.com/2011-01-14/india/28369135_1_temperature-degrees-warmest-year (accessed 20 March 2013).

Weaver, A. (2008) *Keeping our cool: Canada in a warming world*, Toronto: Penguin.

Whiteley, W. (2011) Modelling for life, *For the Learning of Mathematics*, 31(2) 18–19.

Food

Jan Winter

This chapter will look at food issues from two perspectives – the global and the personal. This provides the opportunity to consider the sustainability issues raised by food production for the world's population as well as the personal impact of individuals' food choices on the planet. The first of these perspectives involves consideration of issues around world food production, population, environmental impacts and sustainability. The second involves personal understanding of food issues and their direct impact on individuals. Each perspective is considered in the light of the understandings that students might gain through a critical mathematics education as outlined in the opening chapter.

Global food production and population size

First, global food production and population: there are mathematical issues here about modelling and the kinds of predictions that have been made about the food shortages that would follow population growth. While it could be argued that the mass starvation that was predicted some decades ago has not happened, it could also be the case that there is limited understanding of the real impacts of hunger and poverty on very large numbers of people. Food security has become the focus for much of the analysis of this issue (ODI 2009; IFPRI 2010). Development potential seems limited by food issues as well as by other factors and globalisation has implications for land use in less developed countries: if multinational corporations buy African land for growing agrofuels then that land is not available for local food production (FoEE 2010). The old models of colonisation practised by European countries in the nineteenth and twentieth centuries are being replaced by strategic resource acquisition by countries keen to secure land, and thus increase capacity for food production, beyond their own borders. This may have positive impacts in the countries where land is being sold, as foreign investment offers jobs and capital, or negative ones as land is taken out of the local food production system, making it harder to achieve food self-sufficiency.

Climate change will also have impacts on food production, e.g., desertification, unstable weather patterns, shifts in climate zones and associated ecosystems. In all of these issues, mathematical assumptions underlie the way they are presented and have an impact on the conclusions that are drawn. A critical mathematics education approach can give students the tools to examine these assumptions, drawing on both *technological* and *reflective knowing* (Skovsmose 1994). In terms of the issues discussed in this chapter, mathematical knowing concerns the mathematics used to make the calculations presented in the range of reports cited, as well as the decisions made about how to communicate those ideas most clearly and effectively. Technological knowing involves the models devised to combine the wide range of relevant factors so that unfounded claims are not made through the omission of important elements. Reflective knowing involves the awareness that some of the key issues are the formulation of the questions in the first place, the choice to consider what might seem to be irrelevant or minor issues (such as a shift in population from rural to urban locations) and an awareness of the power balance of the players concerned in world food issues.

We began this book by commenting on the landmark of world population rising above seven billion that was reached in 2011. As this figure continues to rise, with nine billion predicted later this century, the challenges of food production will grow too. We already fail to adequately feed large numbers of the world's population and this is likely to remain the case. A 2011 UK Government report states that one billion people currently go hungry, another billion lack necessary minerals and vitamins for health and a further billion substantially overconsume, leading to obesity and its associated health problems (Foresight 2011). This mismatch between production and need therefore affects about half of the world's population. Further, a report from Save the Children estimates that malnutrition is an underlying cause of the deaths of 2.6 million children each year and that globally one in four children is stunted, physically and mentally, because of poor nutrition (Save the Children 2012).

The range of pressures on food production is much wider than the world has previously experienced. These are summarised as follows:

> The global food system will experience an unprecedented confluence of pressures over the next 40 years. On the demand side, global population size will increase from nearly seven billion today to eight billion by 2030, and probably to over nine billion by 2050; many people are likely to be wealthier, creating demand for a more varied, high-quality diet requiring additional resources to produce. On the production side, competition for land, water and energy will intensify, while the effects of climate change will become increasingly apparent. The need to reduce greenhouse gas emissions and adapt to a changing climate will become imperative. Over this period globalisation will continue, exposing the food system to novel economic and political pressures.
>
> (Foresight 2011: 9)

Food production and energy use

The interconnections between food production and climate change are also highlighted in the Foresight report. Food production makes intensive use of carbon-producing technologies, being responsible for 30 per cent of global greenhouse gas emissions. So our development of a sustainable global system of food production in this century needs not only to produce food for two billion (at least) more people but also to do it in a different way. That is a huge challenge, especially given the wide range of competing interests involved. A major question is the extent to which it makes any sense to talk about 'global' solutions to this type of issue in any case. Perhaps small-scale localised solutions are more realistic and empowering?

A small example illustrates the decisions that such food producers and suppliers face. An organic food producer and distributor in the UK comments in a weekly newsletter about 'food miles' and the limitations of this measure of sustainability. He buys oranges from both Spain and South Africa:

> Counterintuitively, because they travel in ships (which are seven times more efficient than HGVs), according to our calculations the environmental impact of transport from South Africa (310g CO2/kg of fruit) is not that much higher than from Spain (240g CO2/kg of fruit). I sense people yawning as I write; my point is that food miles are a very poor measure of environmental impact. Perhaps more interestingly, Ginés' fruit [from Spain] is normally a hundred times better.
>
> (Riverford 2011)

In another newsletter, he discusses the different energy impacts of importing tomatoes from Europe, which can be grown without any heat to produce them, against 'local' UK tomatoes that cannot be grown without heat. The energy costs of the European tomatoes are considerably lower than those of the local ones, despite the transport costs. Clearly, it is difficult to take a simple view of how to make these decisions without the mathematical skills to interpret and weigh up the range of competing arguments.

In the UK, the arguments about organic food production are often emotional ones, with people holding very passionate views. Whether organic food production is seen as the future of sustainable farming or as a lifestyle choice of the wealthy is a hotly contested issue. The Soil Association, the UK's leading organisation devoted to the promotion of organic food, describes itself as 'the leading UK charity dedicated to promoting sustainable, climate friendly food and farming' (Soil Association 2011) thereby clearly making the link that they and others perceive between organic food and sustainability. In justifying the need for organic food production, their website states the following two principles to illustrate this link:

- Food production should conserve and enhance terrestrial and marine ecosystems and natural resources including soil, water and air.
- Food should be produced, processed, distributed and disposed of in ways that minimise both its local and global ecological footprint.

(Soil Association n.d.)

What might the impacts of climate change itself be on food production? The key changes that we seem to be able to expect are higher overall temperatures and wider variability in weather patterns. Both of these will have an impact on food production, the first globally and the second locally. Different crops will thrive in higher temperatures, possibly destabilising the patterns of food productions in key areas of the world. Variable weather patterns are causing more extreme events to arise; droughts, floods and storms may all become more common if climate models are accurate. (See Example 2 in Chapter 3 on climate change.)

Food equity issues

The issue of food waste is a major one, with 30 per cent of food globally being estimated to be wasted (Gustavsson *et al.* 2011). The reasons for this are varied, from over-purchasing in rich countries to inadequate infrastructure for transporting food and for preserving it in poor ones.

The Save the Children report, *A life free from hunger* (2012), draws together data from a wide range of published studies on child nutrition to come to its conclusions about annual numbers of deaths and rates of stunting of children. This analysis focuses on the impact on children of what Save the Children call the 'global malnutrition crisis'. They state that this crisis has been developing for many years, going unnoticed during the recent years of financial turmoil in developed countries. Its impact is to undermine the progress of less developed countries because of the effect on the children who will form the next generation of citizens. These children will be less productive and less prepared to improve the economies of their countries. The high levels of child mortality also encourage larger family sizes and therefore, paradoxically, higher population growth. This is an argument strongly focused on economic factors with the aim of sustainable development and growth.

The focus on 'stunting' of children enables the report to take a quantitative view of a measurable attribute of children's growth. The definition of stunting used by a key paper in this research is that children are more than two standard deviations below the World Health Organization (WHO) length- or height-for-age standards median (de Onis *et al.* 2011). There are other less visible factors, such as average IQ as a measure of brain development, that the report considers as contributing to the potential of individuals to live full lives. The WHO is proposing a target of a 40 per cent reduction in childhood stunting by 2022 (Save the Children 2012: 71), thus providing a measurable aim for political action.

The report also draws on the results of a poll conducted in five developing countries. The data, provided in more detail in an accompanying report (GlobeScan 2012), offer an opportunity to consider the statistical methods lying behind the headlines. Polls were conducted in five countries, India, Pakistan, Nigeria, Peru and Bangladesh. These were largely 'face-to-face' interviews with a representative sample from the population except, interestingly, in Bangladesh, where the poll was telephone based. It is stated that in Bangladesh the sample was representative of the mobile phone-using population which accounts for between 80 and 90 per cent of the adult population. This different methodology is not considered further in the reporting of results and it would be interesting to consider what differences it might make to the findings.

There is a difficult issue at the heart of this problem, that it is not necessarily to do with shortage of food. Good nutrition is more complex than just growing enough food. It is about growing the right foods and about distributing them appropriately and affordably. Nigeria, for example, is a country with considerable resources and yet it has high levels of malnourished children. In the GlobeScan survey, 27 per cent of respondents in India and 21 per cent in Pakistan reported that they can never afford to buy food such as meat, milk or vegetables. This highlights the political and social justice aspects of this issue. Even when there is enough food overall, there is not always enough for all individuals.

Future possibilities and engaging students with these

An Oxfam report, *Growing a better future* (2011), uses a wide range of headline statistics to argue for the need for action on global food production. Here is a sample:

- the amount of arable land per head has almost halved since 1960;
- agriculture accounts for up to 30 per cent of worldwide greenhouse gas emissions;
- demand for water will increase by 30 per cent by 2030;
- 40 per cent of the US corn crop ends up in gas tanks instead of stomachs;
- four people in every five lack access to social protection of any kind;
- hunger fell by one-third in Brazil between 2000 and 2007;
- in 2009, global investments in renewables overtook fossil fuel spending for the first time.

The argument is being built here that change is possible, is badly needed and is happening. The figures are used to illustrate the broader issues. It is noticeable how much power a statistic holds if it is presented clearly and simply. The discussion to be had is then whether any accuracy or 'truth' is lost through this simplification. The statistics are all sourced and can be investigated by the reader – encouraging students to do this would help them to develop their critical mathematical capacities. Students could choose one of the 'headlines', investigate the underlying statistics on which it is based and present a report on the extent to which they feel the headline accurately presents the data.

So what does all this imply about the mathematical understanding that students need in order to understand the situation and thus have the potential to act effectively? Scanning through the information presented in the first part of this chapter shows a range of arithmetic content, around percentages, averages, proportions, fractions, etc. Then there are the data handling skills implied in the manipulation and presentation of statistical information. These are examples of Skovsmose's (1994) *technological* knowing. Beyond these, which would be present in most mathematical curricula, we would argue that critical skills are important in being able to step back from the data presented and make decisions about the ways in which the information was obtained and the ways in which choices were made about what was presented. This is a shift into *reflective* knowing and can provide students with tools for understanding a wide range of data that is used to inform and convince them.

A valuable activity would be to look at the narrative accompanying the data and consider whether there are assumptions present that could have influenced the ways in which data was collected. This is not to say that such assumptions are negative, all human interactions are based on them, but if we do not examine them we are not able to make the decision to think in a different way or to look at existing ideas from a new perspective.

An example would be the data in the GlobeScan survey. A range of considerations implicit in the survey could be discussed. Why were the particular countries on which the survey focused chosen? Why were questions asked in the way that they were? Are there any issues about possible interpretation of questions that might lead to different responses from people in the same situation? What impact might the different methods of data collection have had? (The case of Bangladesh is interesting. Could the data have been *more* representative through mobile phone sampling given the possible difficulty of travelling to some areas?) What about the way the data are presented and the comparisons drawn out from them? What conclusions might we draw that are not presented in the survey report and why might we have chosen a different perspective? In the classroom, this could begin with a discussion of these questions and then be focused through students choosing a particular aspect of the report and critiquing the mathematical techniques used in its preparation and presentation.

From global to personal – understanding food labelling

The reflective responses to data offered above are a key part of learning about the impact of statistics on our world. They lead on to a consideration of how mathematics shapes the world through its presentation. It is only in the last century that we have developed the technological capacities to feel part of a globalised 'community' and thus to try to understand our impact individually on the world. This is a daunting prospect and may be beyond the reach of individuals, but it leads to the second focus of this chapter, that of personal understanding of food issues. There are several facets to this, including food labelling, individual nutritional needs and links between food consumption and poverty in developed countries. Individual food consumption is influenced by many factors in developed countries and the increase in obesity is an indication that these are not being effectively balanced at present. Taking personal control over food use is a first step in making decisions that may be necessary in developing a global food system that can work in meeting the changing needs identified above.

There has been debate, in the UK, about what type of nutrition labelling is more accessible percentage of daily recommended amounts versus green/amber/red labelling. What is the mathematical basis for the conclusions? What evidence do we have of understanding of different systems and the impact on behaviour? Understanding the *formatting power* of mathematics (Skovsmose 1994) helps us to understand the modelling behind these decisions and therefore consider them more critically.

Table 4.1 Chocolate wrapper labelling

Be treatwise – Get to know your GDAs								
EACH BAG CONTAINS...					GDA Children 5-10 years	Typical values	Per 100g	Per bag
Calories	Sugars	Fat	Saturates	Salt	1800 kcal	Energy kj	2205kj	705kj
170	18.1g	9.6g	6.0g	0.08g	24g	Protein	7.5g	2.4g
					220g	Carbohydrate	56.8g	18.2g
9.4%	21.3%	13.7%	30.0%	2.0%	85g	(of which sugars)	56.6g	18.1g
					70g	Fat	30g	9.6g
... OF YOUR GUIDELINE DAILY AMOUNT (GDA)					20g	(of which saturates)	18.6g	6.0g
To be enjoyed as part of a healthy active lifestyle					15g	Fibre	0.7g	0.2g
					1.4g	Sodium*	0.1g	0.03g
					4g	*Equivalent as salt	0.25g	0.08g
To learn more visit www.betreatwise.org.uk								

A packet of chocolate buttons has the following information on the front:

Calories 170 per bag. 9.4% of child's GDA (Guideline Daily Amount)

This is expanded on the back of the packet (Table 4.1).

This rich collection of data raises many questions about its accessibility and usefulness. Is it intended to be understood by a child (the nutritional baselines given are for a child of between five and ten years old) or a parent? It could be argued that many adults would find it difficult to assess the importance of some of the information here. There are some points to draw out of the data:

- Were a child to consume only chocolate buttons (not recommended!), their entire GDA in calories would be just over ten of these small (32g) packets.
- Similarly, their entire GDA of sugars would be in about five packets, and of saturated fats in about three packets.
- Given these high percentages of these food groups it might seem difficult to parents to estimate whether one of these packets is a reasonable addition to a child's food intake on a given day. How should such 'treats', as the manufacturer describes them, be 'rationed' in a healthy diet?

The UK government promotes a different system of nutritional labelling, using 'traffic lights' to indicate high, medium and low levels of nutritional groups in a product. In this system sugars, fats, saturates and salt are rated and the amount of each food group per serving is given.

Table 4.2   Traffic light labelling ranges (in real life, represented by red, amber, green)

	Sugars	Fat	Saturates	Salt
High (per 100g)	Over 15g	Over 20g	Over 5g	Over 1.5g
Medium (per 100g)	Between 5g and 15g	Between 3g and 20g	Between 1.5g and 5g	Between 0.3g and 1.5g
Low (per 100g)	5g and below	3g and below	1.5g and below	0.3g and below

The ranges for each category are in Table 4.2.

So for example, the chocolate buttons above (for a 32g packet) would be labelled as follows:

Table 4.3   Chocolate wrapper data using traffic light labelling. (The labelling provides information about amounts of each food group per serving, not per 100g)

Sugars	Fat	Saturates	Salt
High	High	High	Low
18.1g	9.6g	6.0g	0.08g

The manufacturers who choose not to use the government's approved system are giving *more* information than recommended, but may feel they are presenting a more neutral picture than the three 'red lights' above give. A confectionery manufacturer could be faced with labelling virtually all their products with three 'red lights' (and the salt content only just falls below the 'amber' range too) which would be an unattractive prospect in marketing terms. Other manufacturers might also feel that some foodstuffs (e.g. cheese or butter) are automatically portrayed as 'bad' rather than foods that need to be consumed in moderation.

Research published by the UK Food Standards Agency (2010) indicated a preference for 'traffic light' labelling as shoppers found this easier to assess quickly while shopping. They also found the range of different formats confusing and preferred a consistent format. Researchers found that their respondents, unsurprisingly, 'had varying confidence in terms of numeracy and the manipulation of numerical information to make comparisons.' (ibid: 6). The traffic light colour system was supportive for those who struggled with numeracy or found numerical calculations intimidating (ibid). The variety of schemes was felt to discourage use of information by some.

Food labelling links to the classroom

So, what about the mathematics required to make decisions based on this information? Percentages clearly need to be understood, in terms of whether a food item with a high percentage of a particular foodstuff is an appropriate choice in the diet. But that is quite a subtle decision; as foods are being bought, how reasonable is it to expect the bigger picture of a family's overall diet to be built up? It could be argued that the 'traffic light' labelling is important here; a supermarket trolley full of items with green and amber, with the occasional red, is likely to be the basis of a good diet while the opposite, lots of red labels with few green or amber, could be a problem. So perhaps the labelling system removes the need for mathematical understanding of percentages and GDAs. Most producers' use of neutral colouring, rather than the traffic light system, means shoppers do not have such easy access to the broad picture of the nutritional content of the food they are buying and therefore need to be able to understand the raw data of percentages.

Students could work with a range of food labels, bringing items from home. Considering the information provided and calculating various statistics, as has been done above with the chocolate button wrapper, could help to provide them with insight into their own diets as well as providing a meaningful context for work on developing skills.

There is a deeper issue than the straightforward technical skills of calculation involved though. Skovsmose's *formatting* power of mathematics is evident here. Food shopping is no longer about simple choices of ingredients but about considering the information provided by the labelling, through models designed by others. We need to evaluate the information we are given to make choices and this information is 'pre-digested' for us to some extent, so that our choices are directed by motives other than our existing knowledge about our preferences for particular foods, our budget or who we will be cooking for. We will be influenced by government and/or producers' choices about how to present information to us and our world is changed as a result. There is a complex interplay between regulation by governments and marketing by food producers and retailers that illustrates the power struggle between different interests. The focus on continual growth in turnover and profits by major retailers has an inevitable conflict with sustainability of production and consumption, as discussed in Chapter 2.

Global and personal – two sides of the same issue

Children suffering from stunting due to malnutrition, as discussed in the earlier part of this chapter, may not have these issues to consider, but are nonetheless subject to the physical and developmental problems associated with inadequate food supplies and not enough of the key nutrients for strong growth. So the populations of both developed and developing countries are, in different ways, dealing with the implications of inappropriate nutrition. These conflicting situations present fertile opportunities for engagement with mathematics in a context of real global concern.

Globalisation is a seemingly unstoppable change that presents new challenges to future 'citizens of the world'. Developing students' critical mathematical skills, their reflective knowing and their sense of the rights of all people may help them to play a positive part in these changes.

References

de Onis, M., Blossne, M., and Borghi, E. (2011) Prevalence of stunting among pre-school children 1990–2020. Growth Assessment and Surveillance Unit, *Public Health Nutrition*, July, 14: 1–7.

Foresight (2011) *The future of food and farming: executive summary.* London: The Government Office for Science.

Friends of the Earth Europe (FoEE) (2010) *Africa: Up for grabs.* Available online at http://www.foeeurope.org/sites/default/files/publications/FoEE_Africa_up_for_grabs_0910.pdf (accessed 17 May 2011).

GlobeScan (2012) Multi-Country Nutrition Poll 2011 Topline Report. London: Save the Children. Available online at http://www.globescan.com/component/edocman/?view=category&id=3&Itemid=591 (accessed 17 January 2012).

Gustavsson, J., Cederberg, C., and Sonesson, U. (2011) *Global food losses and food waste.* Rome: Food and Agriculture Organisation of the UN.

International Food Policy Research Institute (IFPRI) (2010) *Five steps to prevent a repeat of the 2007–08 food crisis.* Washington, DC: IFPRI.

ODI (2009) Climate change, water and food security. Available online at http://www.odi.org.uk/search/site/climate%20change%2C%20water%20and%20food%20security (accessed 12 April 2012).

Oxfam (2011) Growing a better future, Oxford: Oxfam UK. Available online at http://policy-practice.oxfam.org.uk/publications/growing-a-better-future-food-justice-in-a-resource-constrained-world-132373 (accessed 1 April 2012).

Riverford (2001) *Newsletter no.546.* Buckfastleigh: Riverford Ltd.

Save the Children (2012) *A life free from hunger.* London: Save the Children.

Skovsmose, O. (1994) *Towards a philosophy of critical mathematics education*, Dordrecht: Kluwer.

Soil Association (2011) Publicity brochure, Bristol: Soil Association.

Soil Association (n.d.) Environmental sustainability. Available online at http://www.soilassociation.org/sustainablefoodcities/thefivethemes/environmentalsustainability (accessed 23 February 2013).

UK Food Standards Agency (2010) *Citizens' forums on food: Front of pack (FoP) nutrition labelling.* Available online at http://www.food.gov.uk/multimedia/pdfs/citforumfop.pdf (accessed 23 April 2012).

Biodiversity

Alf Coles

The precise nature of biodiversity will be critiqued throughout this chapter. For now it can be taken to be a measure of the abundance of species in a given area. In 1992, leaders of 183 countries pledged under the Convention on Biological Diversity (CBD) to reduce the rate of biodiversity loss by 2010. There was an acceptance that biodiversity loss cannot be reversed in the near future, but the hope was to slow down the rate of loss. Unfortunately, these good intentions seem to have been insufficient: a recent report compiling a group of 31 indicators of biodiversity concludes 'at the global scale it is highly unlikely the 2010 target has been met' (Butchart *et al.* 2010: 1168). In other words, the rate of loss has not been reduced, and in some cases has accelerated. Such statistics have led some scientists (Simpson 2002) to label this time as the sixth period of mass extinction of the planet. The loss of biodiversity raises important questions for life on the planet:

- How bad is the current rate of biodiversity loss?
- Is the loss of biodiversity a risk to human life?
- If biodiversity is to be preserved, where should this happen? And who should pay?
- What is the economic value of biodiversity?
- How is biodiversity linked to poverty?

Loss of biodiversity may compromise the very presence of human life on the planet. Therefore, answers to these questions, and the policy decisions that will be taken in response, could not be more vital. In this chapter, the focus is on the rate of biodiversity loss from a critical mathematics perspective. This critical perspective entails asking: how has mathematics helped shape the crisis of biodiversity loss? How is mathematics used to describe or model biodiversity? What are the ethical social consequences of the use of mathematics in the context of measuring biodiversity?

How mathematics has helped shape the crisis

There are many examples in relation to biodiversity where the use, or perhaps misuse, of mathematics has contributed to species loss. An obvious example is that, following the CBD in 1992, it took until 2006 to reach agreement on a framework of 22 measures of biodiversity with which to measure progress. This lack of consensus about the *mathematics* contributed to years of relative inaction, since there was no agreement on the scale of the problem and hence on the scale of action needed to address the problem.

Another, more specific, example of the misuse of mathematics concerns estimates of the annual global fish catch. Global fish catch, as measured by the Food and Agriculture Organization of the United Nations (FAO), was reported to be increasing between the early 1970s and the late 1980s and, following a dip in the early 1990s, increased again until 1997, reaching a figure of 122 million tonnes (from commercial fishing and aquaculture production). Such figures inevitably encouraged investment in fishing and the sense that it was permissible to continue to increase the overall fish catch. Yet over the same period, there were local examples of drastic collapses in fish biodiversity (see below for more detail on the case of Newfoundland cod). Such discrepancies between official global figures and local experience led two academics, Reg Watson and Daniel Pauly, to investigate the global figures in more detail. They found strong evidence that the rising trend was a mirage, particularly in the 1990s, caused by Chinese over-estimates of their annual fish catch (Watson and Pauly 2001: 534). Watson and Pauly suggest that the Chinese figures may have been influenced by a government directive to increase fish catch, rather than being based on any sound evidence from the industry. Following a directive not to increase fish catch further, official annual figures from China have flat-lined, which leads Watson and Pauly (2001) to continue to doubt their figures. In Watson and Pauly's (2001) corrected data, it appears that the global fish catch has been falling since the late 1980s. Chinese authorities have disputed these claims. In 2008, China reduced by 13 per cent its estimated fish capture figure for the preceding year. In response, the FAO revised down the historical figures for Chinese fish production in the period 1997–2005, resulting in a 2 per cent drop in global fish capture estimates (FAO n.d.). Watson and Pauly estimate that during the 1990s, rather than the official figure of an annual increase of 300,000 tonnes a year in fish catch, the reality may have been a decrease by as much as 350,000 tonnes each year. Again, it seems a decade of inaction may have resulted from an incorrect mathematical picture of the crisis.

In both the lack of consensus on measures of biodiversity and inaccuracies in global fish catch figures, we can see political influence on the use made of mathematical models and data. Disagreements about how, mathematically, to measure biodiversity mask broader disagreements about the desired extent of restrictions on activities that generate income and jobs but are harmful to biodiversity. Manipulation of fish catch data perhaps serves to protect the short-term interests of those in the fishing industry wanting to increase production. Of course, the longer-term interests of those who fight restrictions may well not be compatible with their own short-term ambitions, illustrated vividly in the collapse of the once abundant Newfoundland cod.

Newfoundland cod collapse

The fish stocks of Newfoundland are believed to have once been the largest and most prolific in the world. These stocks were first fished at the beginning of the sixteenth century. Historical estimates of catch levels suggest that from 1875 to 1950 up to 300,000 tonnes of cod were caught every year. This catch was the basis of both the economy and society in Newfoundland. Most of this catch was fished using small boats, harboured in hundreds of Newfoundland communities, during the seasonal migration of the cod. From the 1960s, foreign trawlers were allowed to fish these areas. The increasing mechanization and size of these ships led initially to vastly increased catches (of up to 800,000 tonnes a year). Concerns were expressed at the sustainability of these levels when catch levels began to drop and, in 1977, foreign vessels were banned from the waters off Newfoundland. It appeared that this measure was successful and, in the late 1980s, there were reports that fish numbers were rising (Alverson *et al.* 1987). However, this resurgence was short-lived and, in 1992, the government of Canada was forced to call a moratorium on cod fishing (that persists to the time of writing), after it was estimated that the amount of fish had reduced to 1 per cent of its earlier biomass, a figure from which the cod have hardly recovered. How did this catastrophic collapse occur?

It is intriguing to go back to the Alverson *et al.* report on cod numbers from 1987. The report was published five years before the moratorium was announced. In the executive summary they suggest:

> Estimates of the growth of the total stock may have been overly optimistic, and although we conclude that the total stock has increased since 1977, it has not reached expected levels.
>
> (Alverson *et al.* 1987: 1)

Despite their conclusion that fish stocks were increasing, Alverson *et al.* express serious concerns about the process by which stocks are calculated and allocations granted:

> as a result of the consistent over-estimation of the current stock size, the fishing mortality actually exerted has been consistently in excess of target mortality.
>
> (ibid: 61–2)

Fishing mortality (F) is defined in the following equation:

Total weight of catch = F × total biomass of stock

In other words, F is the proportion of the total fish stock caught in any one year. Once the total catch in a given year is approximated, an estimate can be made of F, in order to arrive at an estimate of the total stock. For a number of years, a target value labelled 'F0.1' was set by the Canadian government; in other words, the aim was to catch 10 per cent of the total biomass. Alverson *et al.*, comment:

> The choice of F0.1 seems to have been arbitrary, or a continuation of the ICNAF [International Commission for the Northwest Atlantic Fisheries] target without any examination of whether the target of an international body is necessarily appropriate for Canada.
>
> (ibid: 73)

However, not only was this figure chosen relatively arbitrarily, but when it came to calculating whether the target was met or exceeded:

> estimates of fishing mortality rate, population size and biomass in the most recent years depends to an ever increasing extent on the value of fishing mortality used for the last year.
>
> (ibid: 32)

And while the estimates of stock size depended on the value of F in the previous year:

> It is generally accepted ... that there is no internal evidence ... that enables discrimination to be made between ... different options concerning the value of F in the last year.
>
> (ibid: 33)

Putting these statements together, it appears that there is no internal evidence that enables distinctions to be made between different options concerning the estimates of stock size. Alverson *et al.* (1987) continue in their critique of the value of F estimated to have taken place in a given year (known as terminal F):

> The choice of terminal F was in the 1970s a subjective matter ... there must have been considerable pressures to adopt a low value of F ... Some echo of these pressures can perhaps be detected in the NAFO [Northwest Atlantic Fisheries Organisation] reports even in 1985 in phrases such as 'concern was expressed about the procedures used ...'
>
> (ibid: 36)

As part of their report, Alverson *et al.* went back through recent data in order to 'tune' the value of F in previous years.

> It is notable that the results obtained yield exploitation rates (F) higher than those [previously] obtained ... and thus we feel that the prior series of ... results may have underestimated fishing mortality in past years.
>
> (ibid: 36)

As in the cases of agreeing on measures of biodiversity and of Chinese fishing figures, there is political interference evident here in the way mathematics is used. By implication, we should perhaps be wary and critical of any statistic being used in a political context. Given the social and economic reliance on fishing of the entire Newfoundland coastal region, presumably it would have been a brave politician who suggested curbing the industry in the 1980s when it appeared that stocks were rising. Yet, by under-estimating the proportion of the total population caught each year (reporting a value of F0.1), fish stocks were consistently over-estimated and, since current values are based on previous ones, errors get compounded. In the case of Newfoundland cod it is almost as though the mathematical model, of catch size, mortality and stock size, masks the uncertainty in the figures and the biases in the data collection. Perhaps writing and talking about 'F0.1' sounds more dispassionately accurate, more scientific, than conveying the human subjectivity, choice and political influence that went into the figure, both as a target and terminal value, assigned for any given year.

However, it is certainly not obvious how to go about capturing the biodiversity in an ocean and the next section looks into some of the most commonly used measures.

How mathematics is used to describe or model the crisis

Having seen some of the ways that mathematics has helped to shape the crisis of species loss, it is worth standing back and reflecting on potential difficulties with measuring biodiversity. This is a question that could potentially be a stimulus for work in school.

Students could be challenged to compare the biodiversity of three areas of the school campus or surrounding area (they can choose the size of area to compare and the location, but perhaps need to compare at least *three* sites). As part of their work, they would need to decide how to measure the biodiversity and explain their approach. Students may be able to collect data over time with the aim of making some recommendations for supporting biodiversity in the area.

To engage in this task, students would first need to decide how to define biodiversity (they could choose to look at animal or plant life, or both). Can they come up with a method for giving a *value* to the biodiversity of each of the three areas? (The simplest idea would be to simply count the number of species in a given area; or biodiversity values could be based on an estimate of how many individuals from each species there are in an area, or an estimate of the total weights of each species). Students may want to try out a range of possible ideas. Having made these decisions, they should be in a position to decide what data they need to collect in each area. Once they have some data, they should be able to rank their areas in terms of diversity.

A task such as the one above would involve decisions about data collection over time and then a consideration of how to make sense of that data. A starting point for collecting any information about biodiversity must be some kind of animal or plant count. This data, collected over time or in different areas, may give an interesting picture of the state of wildlife around the school. It might be particularly interesting if there is a more wild area of the school grounds.

There are potential problems extrapolating species counts to other similar areas. If I come across an anthill or wasps' nest in the area in which I take my data and then extrapolate to the whole region, I may get a vast over-estimate. If plants are considered, it is not at all obvious how to count, for example, an area of grass with one daisy; is this simply two species? Estimates of biomass of each species are perhaps more relevant in this kind of instance. Of course, it becomes even more complicated if species cannot be seen, for example if they are microscopic, underground or underwater.

To deal with species counts in the seas, one method that can be used to measure fish populations is to capture and tag a certain number of a particular species. If we assume that these tagged fish spread themselves evenly throughout the whole population, then if it is possible to find out how many tagged fish are caught in a particular fishing season, an estimate can be made of the whole population. For example, if 500 fish are tagged and 10 are subsequently caught, since 1/50th of the tagged fish are caught, we can estimate that the 500 tagged fish make up 1/50th of the whole population. So, the whole population would be $500 \times 50 = 25,000$ fish. This is called a capture/re-capture method. When done for real, account has to be taken of tags falling off, mortality induced by tagging and tagged fish that are caught but not reported. This method could be adapted to form a possible activity in school, as discussed below.

Imagine you want to find a way to estimate the total number of a given species of fish. We can model this situation by asking, can you find a way to estimate the total number of lentils in a jar? (As a teacher, you would need to bring in a real jar. Each lentil represents one fish of this particular species and the opaque jar signifies the fact that you cannot see them.) You can open the lid only to take samples (of, say, up to 20 lentils), mark them if you want and then replace them (this would be equivalent to taking a vessel into the ocean and catching fish, tagging them if you want and then replacing them). Try not to take account of the size, weight and proportion filled of the jar, as in the real situation you would not have any equivalent information.

One method for doing this task, with lentils, would be to take out twenty, mark them in some way, replace them and then do a series of samples. The number of marked lentils in the samples will make it possible to estimate the total, using a capture/re-capture method.

However, the difficulties with saying something about biodiversity do not end with measurement. Having collected data on the number or weight of different species, it is then not obvious what we might mean by the biodiversity. If we are simply interested in the number of different species, then it seems obvious that the larger the area we survey, the greater the number of species we will find. If this is the measure of biodiversity, then the larger the area we survey, the greater the biodiversity. Instead, we could take a unit of area and measure biodiversity by the number of species in a given area, which would allow comparisons over time and in different regions. Or, what the early measures of diversity sought to do, we could find a measure of the *relative abundance* of species in a given area. If one species is overly dominant this would be a mark of low relative abundance; the more there were equal numbers, the greater the relative abundance.

The first mathematisation of biodiversity came from borrowing models that were originally devised as measures of the information being communicated by radio wave, given the problems of 'noise' generated during the process. The early measures of diversity were the Simpson index and the Shannon index.

The Simpson index is perhaps the simplest and is based on the idea of a weighted average. Having conducted a sample of species in a given area, results (either taking numbers of each species, or biomass) can be divided by their total, to give proportions of each species: $p_1, p_2, p_3, \cdots, p_n$ (assuming there were n species found). So, an area of grass with a single daisy might have only two species with biomass proportions 0.999 and 0.001.

The arithmetic mean of these proportions would then be: $\frac{1}{2}(0.999 + 0.001) = \frac{1}{2}$

In general, the arithmetic mean: $\frac{1}{n} \times (p_1 + p_2 + p_3 + \cdots + p_n)$ will always give the value $\frac{1}{n}$ since the sum of the proportions: $p_1 + p_2 + p_3 + \cdots + p_n$ is, by definition, 1; hence this is not a particularly useful measure of biodiversity.

The basis of the Simpson index is to take a *weighted* arithmetic mean, where the values (p_i) are each multiplied by a number (the 'weight') and divided by the sum of these weights. Weights are chosen to reflect the relative significance of the different values. For example, in calculating the cost of household living, changes in the prices of mortgages, clothes, food will be weighted to reflect the different amounts of money typically spent on these items; a five per cent rise in mortgage rates will be more significant to households than a five per cent rise in postage costs. In the case of measuring relative abundance, the proportions of each species are weighted by their own proportion (i.e., if one species has a high proportion, it becomes more significant in terms of measuring relative abundance).

This weighted mean is therefore:

$$\frac{p_1 \times p_1 + p_2 \times p_2 + p_3 \times p_3 + \cdots + p_n \times p_n}{p_1 + p_2 + p_3 + \cdots + p_n}$$

Remembering that $p_1 + p_2 + p_3 + \cdots + p_n = 1$, this weighted mean, q, is Simpson's index:

$$q = p_1^2 + p_2^2 + p_3^2 + \cdots + p_n^2$$

It is worthwhile here pausing to consider what features of an ecosystem this weighted mean (Simpson's index) will capture. If all species are equally abundant then $p_i = \frac{1}{n}$, for $i = 1$ to n. Hence:

$$q = n \times \left(\frac{1}{n}\right)^2 \text{ and so } q = \frac{1}{n}$$

At the other extreme, if almost all creatures in an ecosystem are from one species, there will be one value of p_i close to 1 with all the others close to zero. Hence, once these values are squared and added, $q \approx 1$. In other words, the closer to 1 the index, the worse the situation in terms of future biodiversity and the closer to zero, the greater the 'polydominance' of different species.

Various other measures are linked to the Simpson index. For example, the Simpson index *of diversity* is defined as $1/q$. The lower the value of q (indicating high biodiversity), the higher this index of diversity. Another measure is the Gini-Simpson index, which is defined as $1-q$, where the lower the value of q, the closer this index gets to 1.

Whereas the Simpson index is a 'weighted arithmetic mean' of the proportions of each species in a sample (weighted by their abundance), the Shannon index is linked to the weighted *geometric* mean. The definition of the geometric mean of a set of n numbers is the nth root of those numbers multiplied together. So the geometric mean, G, of $p_1, p_2, p_3, \cdots, p_n$ is:

$$G = \sqrt[n]{p_1 p_2 p_3 \cdots p_n}$$
$$G = \left[p_1 p_2 p_3 \cdots p_n\right]^{\frac{1}{n}}$$

Weighting the arithmetic mean was done by multiplying values by the weights and dividing by the sum of the weights. Weighting the geometric mean comes from doing the analogous processes for multiplication. In other words, we raise each proportion to the power of the weight and take the kth root, where k is the sum of the weights.

As before, we want to weight species proportions by those proportions themselves. Hence, the weighted geometric mean, M, is:

$$M = \sqrt[n]{p_1^{p_1} p_2^{p_2} p_3^{p_3} \cdots p_n^{p_n}} \text{ where } k = p_1 + p_2 + p_3 + \ldots + p_n$$

Since we know that $k=1$ (the sum of the proportions):

$$M = p_1^{p_1} p_2^{p_2} p_3^{p_3} \cdots p_n^{p_n}$$

As with the earlier arithmetic measure, q, the greater the diversity, the smaller the value of M. A single dominant species indicates M has a maximum value of 1^1 which is 1. Perhaps to make the measure behave more intuitively, Shannon used $\frac{1}{M}$; the greater the biodiversity, the greater the value of $\frac{1}{M}$ – the closer to 1, the more dominant is a single species. This expression ($\frac{1}{M}$) was suggested by Hill (1973) as a measure of diversity; in fact, Shannon defined his diversity index (which he labelled H) as the *logarithm* of ($\frac{1}{M}$). The bigger the number of species, the higher the value of H. In other words, the Shannon index of diversity (as with the Simpson index of diversity) captures the relative abundance of species and their number. The Shannon index of diversity is the most commonly used measure of biodiversity.

The relevance of these indices, for the purposes of this chapter, is what they can tell us about changes in diversity. However, it is precisely in this crucial area, of how these measures can alert us to dangerous or catastrophic biodiversity loss, that some measures can fail to respond adequately. Chao and Jost (forthcoming) ask us to imagine a diverse community with a million equally common species. Taking the Simpson index:

$$q = 1,000,000 \times (1/1,000,000)^2 = 0.000001$$

So, in this community, the Gini–Simpson index, $1-q$, is 0.999999, now imagine …

> A plague attacks this community and eliminates 99.99% of the species, leaving only a hundred species untouched. Ecologists and conservation biologists would consider this a huge drop in diversity, both in terms of the variety of interactions experienced by a constituent organism before and after the plague, and in terms of the conservation value of the pre- versus post-plague communities. The tools of diversity analysis should be able to clearly indicate the magnitude of this drop if they are to be useful in less dramatic situations. Yet the post-plague community's Gini–Simpson index is 0.99, only 1% less than the Gini–Simpson index of the pre-plague community. An ecologist equating the Gini–Simpson index with 'diversity' would therefore conclude that the plague which killed almost all the species did not have a big effect on the community's 'diversity'!
>
> (Chao and Jost, forthcoming)

In a different context, a less significant change in a community can result in bigger changes in the Gini–Simpson index. Taking up the story of this imagined community, now with one hundred equally abundant species, the Gini–Simpson index is 0.99; imagine ninety species remain at constant levels and ten species increase their numbers tenfold. The proportions of the one hundred species, instead of all being 0.01, now change. The ninety that have stayed the same have proportion 0.005 and the ten species to have increased have a proportion of 0.053.

Now, $q = 90 \times (0.005)^2 + 10 \times (0.053)^2 = 0.03034$

Hence, the Gini–Simpson index $(1-q)$ is 0.970, which is a change of around two per cent from 0.99. Compare this percentage change with the one per cent change upon destruction of 99.99 per cent of the one million species. This is evidence that the statistical significance of a change in the Gini–Simpson index may not capture the significance of changes in the actual ecosystem. Yet, Chao and Jost report that it is common in the literature on diversity that when considering changes in these indices, 'the statistical significance of the result is the final product of a study' (Chao and Jost, forthcoming). Yet as we have just seen:

> The statistical significance of a change in the diversity index has little to do with the actual magnitude or biological significance of the change, which is the really important scientific question … The aspects of compositional complexity measured by these indices are not good matches for what most biologists mean by 'diversity', and do not help us judge the real magnitude of an effect.
>
> (Chao and Jost, forthcoming)

In fact, the Simpson diversity index ($\frac{1}{q}$) behaves much more reasonably in the hypothetical circumstances above (this index reduces by the same value as the percentage of species lost, 99.99 per cent, in the plague example). The Shannon index of diversity gives a value of 13.82 for the community of one million equally numerous species, i.e., $-\ln(1/1000000)$. This reduces to $-\ln(1/100) = 4.61$ after the plague, i.e., a reduction of 67 per cent, again a much more reasonable reduction than the Gini–Simpson index.

In an article from 1973 (Hill, 1973) about the mathematics of biodiversity measures, Hill introduced a family of measures, N_a, linked to the proportions of species in a sample (p_i), that unifies measures so far considered in this chapter.

$$N_a = \left(p_1^a + p_2^a + p_3^a + \ldots p_n^a \right)^{\frac{1}{1-a}}$$

Setting $a = 2$, N_2 is the same as $q^{-1} = \dfrac{1}{q}$, the reciprocal of the weighted arithmetic mean, or the Simpson index of diversity. Setting $a=1$ poses a difficulty because the bracket would be raised to the power of an undefined number. However, it is possible to define:

$$N_1 = \lim_{a \to 1} \left(N_a \right) = \lim_{a \to 1} \left(p_1^a + p_2^a + p_3^a + \ldots p_n^a \right)^{\frac{1}{1-a}}$$

This limit (a proof is supplied in Hill 1973) is equivalent to $\dfrac{1}{M}$, the reciprocal of the weighted geometric mean.

Taking $a = 0$, since $p_i^0 = 1$, $N_0 = n$, the number of species in the sample (irrespective of their proportion). Note that there is no equivalent, in this system, to the Gini-Simpson index, which is perhaps an advantage, given the examples above indicate it is a flawed measure.

On Hill's analysis, several different indices of diversity are in fact closely linked and derive from the same property, N_a, which Hill labels "polydominance". N_2 is the reciprocal of an arithmetic mean of the proportions, N_1 the reciprocal of a geometric mean and, if all proportions are equal, N_0 is the reciprocal of a harmonic mean.

[The harmonic mean of a set of n numbers is, n divided by the sum of the reciprocals of each number, or $\dfrac{n}{\sum \frac{1}{p_i}}$. If each p_i is equal (at $\dfrac{1}{n}$) then $\sum_{i=1}^{n} \frac{1}{p_i} = \sum_{i=1}^{n} \frac{1}{1/n} = \sum_{i=1}^{n} n = n^2$, hence the harmonic mean is $\dfrac{n}{n^2} = \dfrac{1}{n}$.]

In all these measures, the higher the value, the greater the biodiversity. Hill (1973) suggests distinguishing between N_a as indices of diversity and $\ln(N_a)$ as measures of entropy (such as the Shannon's 'H'), which are equivalent but less easy to visualise. He notes that it has been known since at least the time of Pythagoras that the geometric mean always lies between the arithmetic and harmonic means and suggests, for this reason, that N_2 is an unnecessary measure as it will always lie between N_1 and N_0. When looking at the different measures, N_2, N_1, N_0, quite striking similarities are observed in how these measures behave across samples. The fact that these three measures behave so similarly and that they include N_0, the number of species, led Hill to conclude that 'the notion of diversity is little more than the notion of the effective number of species present' (Hill 1973: 431).

Chao and Jost (forthcoming) also use the phrase 'effective number of species', which is taken to mean the number of *polydominant* species that would give a particular diversity index number. If students have engaged in the first task of this chapter, to collect biodiversity data at a range of sites on the school campus, they would be able to calculate N_2, N_1 and N_0 for their data. Students should find that the three measures all give the same rank order for the biodiversity of their areas. They could be given the task to come up with a recommendation for the best measure of biodiversity. They may well come to a similar conclusion as Hill, and Chao and Jost, that the simplest and best measure of biodiversity is based on some kind of species count. If they have collected data over time, they may be able to draw conclusions about how biodiversity is changing in their area.

The lack of agreement and range of different biodiversity measures is an example of some apparently complex mathematics masking what is essentially an easy-to-understand and intuitive notion that the diversity of an ecosystem is the effective number of different species in a given area. Given the essentially similar behaviour, mathematically, of the different measures of diversity (N_a) and the equivalence of the entropy measures (e.g., H), it is even more extraordinary that it took between 1992 and 2006 for a global agreement on measures of diversity in order to begin tracking the evidence of biodiversity loss, to inform global action. This awareness takes us into the realms of reflective knowing, and the political and economic pressures that may influence ostensibly 'pure' mathematical models or decisions. There are now global models of biodiversity that attempt to track and predict the influence of human activity on species loss. One model (GLOBIO 3) takes biodiversity to be 'the remaining mean species abundance (MSA) of original species, relative to their abundance in pristine or primary vegetation' (Alkemade *et al*. 2009: 375). What this means is that species are counted and their abundance is divided by the species count in undisturbed situations. The average of these proportions gives the MSA. So this model uses species counts as the measure of diversity, and works with proportions in order to get a measure of the impact of human activity.

However, it should be noted that some measures of the global situation aim to indicate features of system-relations beyond the counts of species in an area. There is an awareness that biodiversity cannot be studied in isolation, or at least that the effects of biodiversity loss are complex.

Ethical and social consequences of the use of mathematics

Having looked at how mathematics has helped shape the crisis in biodiversity and how it is used to measure and describe biodiversity, the last part of the critical mathematics education approach is to consider the ethical and social consequences of the use of mathematics. These consequences can be appreciated by focusing on the role of the use of mathematics in particular instances, such as, for example, the crisis, already dealt with in this chapter, of the collapse of Canadian cod stocks in 1992. The social upheaval following this collapse is still felt today, since 40,000 people lost their jobs, and cod stocks to date have not recovered. To get any sense of the effects of this upheaval, literature is perhaps of more use than academic reports. Newfoundland is the backdrop for the novel *The Shipping News* by Annie Proulx (1993), written one year after the moratorium on cod fishing; this section ends with three quotations from near the end of that book.

GOOD-BYE TO ALL THAT
There are some days it just doesn't pay to get up. Harold Nightingale of Port Anguish knows this better than anyone. It's been a disastrous fishing season for

Port Anguish fishermen. Harold Nightingale has caught exactly nine cod all season long. 'Two years ago,' he said 'we took 170,000 pounds of cod off Bumpy Banks. This year – less than zero. I dunno what I'm going to do. Take in washing, maybe.'

To get the nine cod Mr. Nightingale spent $423 on gas, $2,150 on licenses, $4,670 on boat repairs and refit, $1,200 on new nets …

(p. 219)

Jack said the cod were small, five or six pounds on average, you rarely got one that went more than fifty nowadays, though in early times men caught great cod of two hundred pounds. Or more. Overfished mercilessly for twenty years until the stocks neared collapse. Did collapse, said Jack, up at the table, his knife working.

'Why I don't stop fishing, see' he said, deftly ripping up, jerking out the entrails, cigarette in the corner of his mouth, 'even if I wanted to, is because I'd never get my licenses for lobster or salmon fishing again. Don't know why, I loves lobster fishing best. You let your cockadoodle license lapse just one season and it's gone forever.'

(p. 292)

'Jesus! You think it can't get worse, it gets worse! This business about allocating fish quotas as if they were rows of potatoes you could dig. If there's no fish you can't allocate them and you can't catch them; if you don't catch them, you can't process them or ship them, you don't have a living for nobody. Nobody understands their crazy rules no more. Stumble along. They say "too many local fishermen for not enough fish." Well, where has the fish gone? To the Russians, the French, the Japs, West Germany, East Germany, Poland, Portugal, the UK, Spain, Romania, Bulgaria – or whatever they call them countries nowadays.

'And even after the limit was set, the inshore was no good. How can the fish come inshore if the trawlers and draggers gets 'em all fifty, a hundred mile out? And the long-liners gets the rest twenty mile out? What's left for the inshore fishermen.' Watching Quolye's clumsy work with the knife. 'You got the idea. That's all there is to it. Just keep at it steady.'

(p. 292)

Conclusion

We are at pains not to paint too bleak a picture of the state of the planet in this book and there are some positive developments in the case of global fish stocks. There are examples of fish stock recovery, following fishing bans or reductions, and there is now a global consensus on the need to address the loss of fish numbers (in 2002, at the Johannesburg World Summit on Sustainable Development, world leaders committed to restoring fish stock to sustainable yield levels by 2015). As with biodiversity, however, the measure of what makes a yield sustainable is contested and complex. There are moves to set up networks of marine reserves (for example, on the Great Barrier Reef) and some evidence that a large network of such reserves can have both environmental and economic benefits. Greenpeace published a report in 2006: *Roadmap to recovery: a global network of marine reserves* setting out a rationale and proposal to dedicate 40 per cent of the world's oceans as reserves. While these zones may have limited impact on highly mobile species (for example, cod), a global network of reserves could be a significant boost to the future of global fish stocks and diversity.

Further reading

- The Food and Agriculture Organization of the United Nations (FAO) homepage offers information about the state of global food sources, for example fish population size: http://www.fao.org/index_en.htm
- The homepage of Lou Jost has links to articles and books on biodiversity: http://www.loujost.com/

References

Alkemade, R., van Oorschot, M., Miles, L., Nellemann, C., Bakkenes, M. and ten Brink, B. (2009) GLOBIO 3: A framework to investigate options for reducing global terrestrial biodiversity loss, *Ecosystems,* 12: 374–90

Alverson, D., Gullard, J., Beamish, F., Larkin, P. and Pope, J. (1987) *A study of the trends of cod stocks off Newfoundland and factors influencing their abundance and availability to the inshore fishery.* Submitted by the Task Group on Newfoundland Inshore fisheries, November. Ottawa: DFO.

Butchart, S., Walpole, M., Collen, B., van Strien, A., Scharlemann, J., Almond, R., Baillie, J., Bomhard, B., Brown, C., Bruno, J., Carpenter, K., Carr, G., Chanson, J., Chenery, A., Csirke, J., Davidson, N., Dentener, F., Foster, M., Galli, A., Galloway, J., Genovesi, P., Gregory, R., Hockings, M., Kapos, V., Lamarque, J-F., Leverington, F., Loh, J., McGeoch, M., McRae, L., Minasyan, A., Morcillo, M., Oldfield, T., Pauly, D., Quader, S., Revenga, C., Sauer, J., Skolnik, B., Spear, D., Stanwell-Smith, D., Stuart, S., Symes, A., Tierney, M., Tyrrell, T., Vié, J-C., and Watson, R. (2010) Global biodiversity: indicators of recent declines, *Science,* 328(5982): 1164–8.

Chao, A. and Jost, L. (forthcoming) *Diversity analysis,* London: CRC Press.

FAO (n.d.) Global Capture Production. Available online at http://www.fao.org/fishery/statistics/global-capture-production/en (accessed 1 March 2013).

Hill, M. (1973) Diversity and evenness: a unifying notation and its consequences, *Ecology,* 54(2): 427–32.

Proulx, A. (1993) *The shipping news,* London: Fourth Estate.

Simpson, D. (2002) *What is biodiversity worth? And to whom?* Issue Brief 02 – 16, Washington, DC: Resources for the Future. Available online at http://www.rff.org/Publications/Pages/PublicationDetails.aspx?PublicationID=9618 , (accessed 7 July 2010).

Watson, R. and Pauly, D. (2001) Systematic distortion in world fisheries catch trends, *Nature,* 424: 534–6.

Towards a mathematics for human rights and social justice

Tony Cotton

Introduction

This is a book about mathematics so I would like to invite you to carry out a piece of mathematics at this point. Imagine you were to count out loud from zero to six million starting now. One, two, three, four ... and so on. How long would it take until you finally reached six million? I would like you to carry out this task before you read the next paragraph.

I often set this as an activity with beginning teachers or pupils that I am working with. The smallest answer we have ever been given is 69 days, and this assumes you can read out a number such as 5,435,682 in one second (which you cannot), and that you can carry on counting for over two months without sleeping, which you cannot either. I have asked many groups of students to carry out this rather trivial piece of mathematics over the years before reminding them that six million is generally accepted as the number of Jewish people killed in the holocaust. A colleague of mine, a mathematics educator called Steve Lerman, reminded us that six million meant one thing to him in everyday life, something else as a mathematician, and it was a number deeply related to his identity as a Jew. This is a clear example of how we need mathematics to begin to make sense of a world that on occasions is very difficult to understand. Here mathematics is both describing a world by developing our understanding of 'large numbers' and offering possibilities to act on the world in that we are challenged to use our new knowledge to revisit our understanding of history and act on current injustices which marginalised groups face.

The purpose of this chapter is to discuss the notions of social justice and human rights: these areas may be seen as the ethical dimension of teaching mathematics as if the planet, and those that inhabit it, matter. The first part of the chapter introduces definitions of these concepts and the second half explores the mathematical approaches that may be taken if we accept that these areas are important. In exploring how the learning and teaching of mathematics relates to ideas of social justice and human rights, I refer to the ideas of transformation, reformation and accommodation introduced in Chapter 1.

The opening chapter of this book makes it clear that as a group of authors, we do not see mathematics as a subject discipline that sits outside culture, history and political contexts. The mathematics that is taught in our schools and the teaching and learning strategies that we choose to use are bound up in the content of the mathematics curriculum, the teaching strategies that are acceptable to those who police us, the environment within which we teach and the resources we draw on.

Social justice

John Rawls (1972) offers a thought experiment which can help in any exploration of social justice. Using the concept of a 'veil of ignorance', he asks us to imagine that the world has completely changed whilst we are hidden under this veil. When the veil is removed we have no idea of our position or role in the new society. If the society is a 'socially just' society, no matter what position or role we are now placed in, we will be able to live life to the full. We will be able to live the Aristotelian good life. We can recast this question to explore social justice in and through mathematics education, which is the task of this chapter. Bring to the front of your mind your own children, or children that you love and cherish in a new thought experiment. Can I invite you to imagine a mathematics classroom that you know well or that you work in? I wonder if you would be happy for your child to exchange places with any of the other children in the class. Would they still have access to the life choices and future opportunities that you would want to be available for them? You can repeat this question at institutional level, and at national and international level. One result of asking this question is to notice where injustice lies: which individuals, which groups of individuals and which nations are currently disadvantaged by local, national and international policy and practice. We can then ask the question, how should structures, policies, procedures and practices be changed so as not to disadvantage these groups? So this chapter envisages a mathematics education that sees as one of its aims the creation of a more socially just world. A world in which you would be happy for a child you love to learn in any classroom in any school, and to exchange places with any child in any classroom in any school. The stance here is that a critical mathematics education can empower and liberate individuals by allowing them to take control over their lives. If we regard mathematics as a way of viewing the world then the corollary of this is that the greater our grasp of mathematics, the better able we are to interpret the complexities of the world.

Human rights

The Universal Declaration of Human Rights was first adopted by the United Nations in 1948. There were 30 articles that aimed to ensure that the horrors of the Second

World War would never be repeated. The articles which relate directly to education in general and mathematics education in particular described above include the right to freedom of opinion and expression, including the right to receive and impart information. If we are to form opinions we want to share and if we are to interrogate the information we receive, or wish to impart, we need mathematical understandings that will allow us to interrogate data critically.

Article 26 describes the purpose of education for human rights. This article offers us a way in which we can 'audit' our classroom practices. It states:

> Education shall be directed to the full development of the human personality and to the strengthening of respect for human rights and fundamental freedoms. It shall promote understanding, tolerance and friendship among all nations, racial or religious groups, and shall further the activities of the United Nations for the maintenance of peace.

In 2000, the Millennium Summit revisited the United Nations Declaration of Human Rights and set eight international development goals to be reached by 2015. These eight goals are

Goal 1: Eradicate extreme poverty and hunger
Goal 2: Achieve universal primary education
Goal 3: Promote gender equality and empower women
Goal 4: Reduce child mortality rates
Goal 5: Improve maternal health
Goal 6: Combat HIV/AIDS, malaria, and other diseases
Goal 7: Ensure environmental sustainability
Goal 8: Develop a global partnership for development

These goals offer us areas to explore in two ways. Mathematics classrooms are ideal sites to evaluate the data that can tell us how close we are to meeting the targets which go alongside the goals. Secondly we can examine how our own classroom practices work towards environmental sustainability and build global partnerships. These areas are explored in more detail in other chapters in this book.

Having outlined the view of social justice and human rights on which I draw, I will now move to look specifically at each concept and how the learning and teaching of mathematics can contribute to both social justice and human rights.

Mathematics for social justice

In order to explore issues around social justice, I will take as a starting point the work of Richard Wilkinson and Kate Pickett in *The Spirit Level* (2009). This book outlines the mathematics they have used to argue that greater equality, in terms of income, leads to increased health and wellbeing in the population. They plot the level of health-related/social problems against the difference in income of the world's 20 richest countries and 50 states in the USA. They show that when there is large differential in the income scale then drug abuse, alcohol abuse, obesity, mental health problems, and even teenage pregnancy occur more frequently, people live for a shorter period and more people commit suicide. They also show that Scandinavia and Japan have the narrowest gap between highest and lowest incomes and the best psychological health for their populations.

The book is pedagogical in that it both acts as a 'teacher' and acts as a resource for teaching. The preface contains an explanation of how to interpret scatter graphs and lines of regression. However, the purpose of the book is not to teach us about data handling and interpreting data. Wilkinson and Pickett are clear about their aim for the text:

> The theory and evidence set out in this book tells us how to make substantial improvements in the quality of life for the vast majority of the population. Yet unless it is possible to change the way most people see the societies they live in the theory will be stillborn. Public opinion will only support the necessary political changes if something like the perspective we outline in this book permeates the public mind.
>
> (2009: xii)

It would be possible to see a book such as this operating as an alternative curriculum. For example, sections of the book explore the topics of 'educational performance', 'teenage births' and 'social mobility'. If we look at these themes in more depth, we can examine how they might impact on our students' understanding of themselves and the world in which they live.

Educational performance

Differential educational performance has been central to political debate across the world. If the group to which we belong or the background from which we come impacts on the outcomes of education, this is seen as inequitable. Reflecting on the Rawlsian view (Rawls 1972) of social justice offered at the opening of the chapter, if our family or economic background acts as a predictor of our success in terms of academic outcomes in school, we could see this as a symptom of an unjust education system. In the Rawlsian sense of social justice, a 'socially just' education system would not disadvantage those already disadvantaged in any society. So, the opening statement of the chapter exploring educational performance reads rather starkly. Wilkinson and Pickett assert:

> Although good schools make a difference, the biggest influence on educational attainment, how well a child performs in school and later in higher education, is family background.
>
> (2009: 103)

This is not an unsupported assertion. Drawing on international data from the Programme for International Student Assessment (PISA), a bank of tests delivered in 43 countries in 2000, combining average scores for reading and mathematics and plotting this against income inequality, they are able to show that maths and literacy scores of 15-year-olds are lower in more unequal countries. That is, countries with the widest disparities in income between the richest and poorest members of society. They also show that the mathematics and literacy scores of eighth-graders are lower in more unequal US states and more children drop out of high school in more unequal US states.

The data has been contested in a pamphlet released by a right-wing think-tank. The pamphlet, entitled *Beware False Prophets* by Peter Saunders (2010), challenges some of the claims made by Wilkinson and Pickett. One facet of current research is the possibility of challenges from outside the scientific community which are not subjected to the same process of peer review but simply placed on websites of political organisations. This should encourage us to develop critical mathematicians who can read research for themselves and make their own minds up about where the truth lies. In this case, Saunders ignores the body of evidence on which *The Spirit Level* is based and his main error is to include very poor countries in his analysis. The main assumption on which *The Spirit Level* is based is that the analysis only applies once the population of a country has reached a minimum standard of living.

In Chapter 1, Richard Barwell offered three purposes for mathematics: accommodation, reformation and transformation. Reformation mathematics is described in the opening chapter as 'relating mathematics to the world in order to refine how things are done'. Drawing on data such as the PISA scores discussed above meets this requirement. In a mathematics classroom, to move beyond the raw data and explore possible changes that could be made is to begin to challenge the inequity which is exposed by the research. A transformative mathematics supports students in analysing and critiquing perspectives that shape how the world is understood. This allows students to see the 'outside world' as the source of 'sustainability' problems. Is there a place in the mathematics classroom to ask 'how might we do things differently?' Can we support students in engaging in action on their world?

A school classroom could be the site for analysis of data such as that provided by Wilkinson and Pickett. Asking critical questions through interpreting data, challenging the interpretations that are offered to us, suggesting solutions and then researching the impact of these solutions (see Chapter 8) allows us to work on Skovsmose's (2009) concept of 'reflective knowing' which is also outlined in the opening chapter. 'Reflective knowing' allows us to focus on how mathematics represents and describes lived experience. It also allows us to focus on how mathematics constructs a reality. The following sections exemplify how we could draw on these ideas in our mathematics classrooms.

Teenage births

There can be a tendency to demonise teenage mothers in the media and the aim of this section is not to offer a simple view of a complex situation. Rather it is to explore how mathematics can help us explore an issue which has an impact on the life chances of groups of young people in our schools. It is important to balance any work on

Table 6.1 Teenage pregnancy rates by income in the UK

Household income	Teenage birth rates
Poorest quartile	4.8%
Second poorest quartile	2.9%
Second richest quartile	2.4%
Richest quartile	1.2%

Source: Wilkinson and Pickett (2009: 122)

early pregnancies with case studies of success stories from families that started in the mother's teenage years.

Babies born to teenage mothers are more likely to be born prematurely with a low birth weight and to be at a higher risk of dying in infancy. These babies are also less likely to succeed as they move through their own education and are at a higher risk of becoming involved in juvenile crime (Wilkinson and Pickett 2009).

To pause for a moment and think about 'reflective knowing', there are many examples of successful and secure families built from 'teenage' births. This may be a lens through which to explore the mathematics here. What does the mathematics tell us about the world in 'general', how does it construct a world in which all teenage mothers are perceived as deviant in some way, and why are there individual stories that sit outside the mathematics?

Table 6.1 shows a gradient in teenage birth rates by household income in the UK. The rate is 4.8 per cent for the poorest quarter of families and 1.2 per cent in the richest quarter. Teenage birth rates are also higher in more unequal countries and teenage pregnancy rates higher in more unequal US states.

It might be appropriate in a mathematics classroom to explore comparative data for the locality in which your school is placed. The data for wards within a single authority in the UK is usually available. A particular town or city in which you work could be compared with the highest and lowest incidences of teenage pregnancies across the country or globe, to offer students a broader picture.

The issues presented here fall into the realm of social justice, as none of us would want to see children we care for more likely to die young or fall into juvenile criminal behaviour. The issues are mathematical as the mathematics is telling us that certain groups are more likely to be at risk of injustice simply because of the family into which they are born. However, we have to move beyond the mathematical data and into the realms of reflective knowing to explore questions such as: why are young women making these choices? How do some young women make a success of this choice? What is the impact on young fathers?

Social mobility

Social mobility is a key idea underpinning social justice. If there is high social mobility, we are able to follow many life choices and these are not dependent on family background or the social situation into which we are born. If there is low social

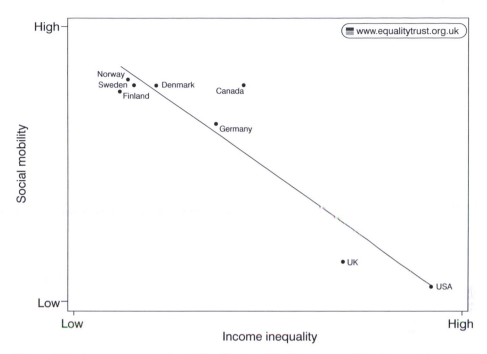

Figure 6.1   Income vs social mobility. Source: http://www.equalitytrust.org.uk/node/410

mobility, background is much more likely to define job prospects, earning potential and the life choices that are available. This is sometimes referred to as equality of opportunity. Measuring social mobility requires longitudinal data to be collected and people's life histories to be heard, explored and analysed; because of this, data is only available on a relatively small number of countries.

The data in Figure 6.1 is confined to the Scandanavian countries, the United Kingdom, the United States, Canada and Germany. Whilst this shows that social mobility is much higher in Scandinavia, Germany and Canada than the UK or the US, it is impossible to link this causally to income equality. Wilkinson and Pickett (2009) draw on other forms of evidence to support the assertion that greater inequality militates against social mobility. Debating whether or not the following three pieces of evidence support this assertion is potentially a worthwhile mathematical task.

First, there is evidence that social mobility is decreasing in both the US and the UK and this has mirrored a widening of the gap between rich and poor in these two countries. Second, if we are to make the assumption that successful educational outcomes support social mobility, then we could look to education spending as a predictor of social mobility. There is data to suggest that the greater the income equality in a country, the more it spends on public education. Finally, Wilkinson and Pickett (2009) point out that in both the UK and the US there is an increasing geographical segregation of rich and poor.

The aim for this section of the chapter has been to exemplify how the 'content' of the curriculum may be impacted if we are to see the study of mathematics as enabling in terms of exploring issues of social justice. I would argue that through the study of such issues, students would come to a more critical understanding of the world in which they live and the world which they are forming. This critical understanding is a precursor for action on the world. The following section revisits this process but with a focus on 'human rights'.

Mathematics for human rights

Earlier in this chapter I suggested that mathematics for human rights operated in two ways. First, to analyse available data, allowing students to assess how close our governments are to meeting the millennium goals. Second, through examining how our own classroom practices work towards human rights through the ethos they encourage and through the extent to which they support environmental sustainability and build global partnerships.

Drawing on the work of Marilyn Frankenstein and her 'Quantitative Reasoning' programme (Frankenstein 1989), I will explore the ways in which issues of employment and unemployment, and AIDS and HIV can be explored in the mathematics classroom. These two areas have direct relevance to human rights and the millennium goals. The latter part of the chapter draws on my previous work with a project entitled Integrating Global and Anti-Racist Perspectives (GARP) within the curriculum to show how issues of human rights can underpin the ethos of our classroom practices.

The central theme for Frankenstein's teaching on her Quantitative Reasoning programme, that she has been teaching since 1978, is using mathematics for peace and justice. This section shows how reasoning quantitatively about public and community issues is connected to using maths to work for justice and to work against injustice. Frankenstein sees her work as a way of bringing about change in the world. She says,

> [this] book helps adults to relearn maths. Rather than teaching maths as something to be reproduced in tests for the teacher, the book encourages students to make maths part of their armoury of skills for interpreting and acting on the world.
>
> (Frankenstein 1989: xvi.)

The contents page of the book looks like any other mathematics text-book, with chapters on 'comparing and rounding fractions' and the meaning of percentages, for example. However, it is the content with which she exemplifies the mathematics that the difference between this volume and a standard mathematics texts becomes evident.

For example, in the chapter which deals with 'Rounding whole numbers and decimal', the following problem appears, using the percentages in Table 6.2. These percentages are out of the total number of black workers in the USA (hence the 100 per cent figure in the top row):

> Unemployment statistics vary depending on who is counted as unemployed. A more comprehensive concept, underemployment, includes
> - unemployed workers looking for work but unable to find a job

- discouraged workers who are are unemployed and want work but who are not actually looking for a job as they believe no jobs are available
- involuntary part-time workers who want full-time work but who are unable to find it
- workers in jobs which provide income inadequate to support a decent standard of living.

Table 6.2 Counting the underemployed, 1975 USA (all numbers in thousands)

	Low Estimate		Middle Estimate		High Estimate	
Workers from the black communities	10,835	100%	11,295	100%	12,049	100%
Unemployed	1,450	13.4%	1,459	12.9%	1,459	12.1%
Discouraged workers	306	2.8%	766	6.8%	1,520	12.6%
Involuntary part-time workers	638	5.9%	638	5.6%	638	5.3%
The working poor	615	5.7%	1,266	11.2%	2,523	21%
Total under employment	3,018	27.8%	4,129	36.6%	6,140	51%

[Table 6.2] … include[s] low, middle and high estimates, which vary according to estimates of the hidden underemployed. Use [Table 6.2] to create and solve five problems whose solutions involve rounding numbers.

(Frankenstein 1989: 156)

Using this sort of data in the mathematics classroom would encourage discussion and debate about the nature of unemployment and underemployment. It would also require a discussion about methods of data collection in addition to focusing on the mathematics itself. In this case, the mathematical focus is to enable students to become familiar with rounding large numbers. Later in the book, Frankenstein (1989: 183) introduces the data in Table 6.3.

Table 6.3 Approximate failure rate of various contraceptives

Method	Actual use failure rate
Hysterectomy	1 out of 1,000,000
Vasectomy	15 out of 10,000
Oral contraceptives (combined)	35 out of 1,000
Condom and spermicide	5 out of 100
IUD (intra-uterine device)	6 out of 100
Condom	175 out of 1,000
Diaphragm	225 out of 1,000
Spermicidal foam	30 out of 100
Rhythm	35 out of 100
Chance	80 out of 100

The data in Table 6.3 is used to illustrate how we can change fractions into decimals, and decimals into percentages for comparison.

Another possibility for working with pupils in our classrooms on mathematics for social justice is to work on the millennium development goals. For example, Millennium Goal 6 states that poverty can be tackled by combating HIV/AIDS, malaria and other diseases, and Target 6A is to have halted the spread of HIV/AIDS by 2015 and begun to reverse the spread of the disease. The 2010 fact sheet from the United Nations offers the following information:

1. Every day over 7,400 people are infected with HIV and 5,500 die from AIDS-related illnesses. HIV remains the leading cause of death among reproductive-age women worldwide.
2. An estimated 33.4 million people were living with HIV in 2008, two-thirds of them in sub-Saharan Africa.
3. Access to HIV treatment in low- and middle-income countries increased tenfold over a span of just five years.
4. Malaria kills a child in the world every 45 seconds. Close to 90 per cent of malaria deaths occur in Africa, where it accounts for a fifth of childhood mortality.
5. 1.8 million people died from tuberculosis in 2008, about 500,000 of whom were HIV-positive.

(United Nations 2010)

It might be appropriate for students in the mathematics classroom to decide what additional data they would need to evaluate the progress made towards Goal 6A. The teacher could support them finding the data and allow the students to carry out the analysis. The World Health Organization provides data on its website which students could analyse and The United Nations statistical division (unstats.un.org/unsd/databases.htm) offers useful data. A fruitful activity would be for groups of pupils to explore this data and prepare a short presentation for the rest of the class on progress towards the meeting the goals.

Conclusion

This chapter has envisaged a mathematics education that sees as one of its aims the creation of a more socially just world. The stance here is that a critical mathematics education can empower and liberate individuals by allowing them to take control over their lives. If we regard mathematics as a way of viewing the world then the corollary of this is that the greater our grasp of mathematics, the better able we are to interpret the complexities of the world.

It seems appropriate to end this chapter with an extract from the open letter to teachers reproduced in Haim Ginott's book, *Teacher and child: a book for parents*.

Dear Teachers:

I am a survivor of a concentration camp. My eyes saw what no person should witness. Gas chambers built by learned engineers. Children poisoned by educated physicians. Infants killed by trained nurses. Women and babies shot and burned by high school and college graduates.

So I am suspicious of education. My request is: help your students become more human. Your efforts must never produce learned monsters, skilled psychopaths, or educated Eichmanns. Reading, writing, and arithmetic are important only if they serve to make our children more human.

(Ginott 1975: 317)

This reminds us that the task of mathematics educators who are teaching as if the planet matters is to support our students to become human through their learning of mathematics, not simply to become efficient and effective mathematicians.

References

Frankenstein, M. (1989) *Relearning mathematics: a different third r – radical maths.* London: Free Association Books.

Ginott, H. (1975) *Teacher and child: a book for parents.* New York: Macmillan.

Rawls, J. (1972) *A theory of justice.* Oxford: Oxford University Press.

Saunders, P. (2010) *Beware false prophets: equality, the good society and* The Spirit Level. London: Policy Exchange.

Skovsmose, O. (2009) *In doubt: about language, mathematics, knowledge and life-worlds.* Rotterdam: Sense Publishers.

Wilkinson, R. and Pickett, K. (2009) *The spirit level: why equality is better for everyone.* London: Penguin Books.

United Nations (1948) Universal declaration of human rights. Available online at http://www.un.org/en/documents/udhr/ (accessed 8/12/12).

United Nations (2000) Millennium development goals. Available online at http://www.un.org/millenniumgoals/index.shtml (accessed 8/12/12).

United Nations (2010) Goal 6: Combat HIV/AIDS, malaria and other diseases. Available online at http://www.un.org/millenniumgoals/pdf/MDG_FS_6_EN.pdf (accessed 8/12/12).

Part II
Into the classroom as if the planet matters

Critical mathematics education
From theory to practice

Tony Cotton

In this second part of the book, we suggest ways that an alternative view of mathematics can be offered through including content that develops students' understanding of environmental issues and draws on resources that use environmental questions as a starting point for problem solving. We will also show that using collaborative teaching strategies can help develop positive and critically aware attitudes towards sustainability. In this part, we take as our starting point specific areas of mathematics and examine ways in which the teaching and learning of these areas can be developed in our classrooms. We hope the moves we offer in this section can provide a genuine alternative, in line with the requirements of 'critical mathematics education' (Skovsmose (1994).

Introduction

This chapter describes the ways in which a dominant worldview of mathematics and its teaching and learning is embedded in the content of the curriculum. I argue that this dominant view is also present in the pedagogical approaches preferred within mathematics classrooms and the environment in which students learn mathematics. I also suggest that the view of mathematics which teachers bring with them to the classroom and the ways in which they measure success in mathematics also act to enculturate students to accept mathematics as distant from issues of sustainability and human rights. The next two sections of this chapter draw on two research projects, one with students in a secondary school in the English Midlands and one with beginning mathematics teachers in the North of England (see Cotton 2008, 2010). These projects examined how subject knowledge is conceptualised and prioritised as the mark of a good teacher: how this can lead to a technicist view of teaching and how it leads to a shared or common sense view of expectations between teachers and students which stifles innovation or any alternative perceptions. The aim is not to present a pessimistic view, but rather to exemplify and accept that in many classrooms mathematics teaching does not proceed 'as if the planet matters'. The final part of this chapter draws on the work of Skovsmose, to offer exemplars of cross-curricular projects which can support teachers in developing an atmosphere of reflection and critique in their classrooms.

Chapter 1 introduced Skovsmose's construction of critical mathematics education and made the link between this notion and an education for sustainability. Skovsmose draws on Henri Giroux, one of the founding theorists of critical pedagogy, to offer a formulation of critical education which suggests that 'schools ... [should] educate students to be critical citizens' who can think, challenge, take risks, and believe that their actions will make a difference to the larger society' (Giroux 1989: 214). From this starting point he defines 'mathemacy' as 'a radical construct ... rooted in the spirit of critique and the project of possibility that enables people to participate in the understanding and transformation of society' (Skovsmose 1994: 27). It is pertinent to note the title of Giroux's work which is *Schooling for Democracy*. This discusses designing education for democracy rather than economic growth. This is a challenge to the dominant view pervading the research reported in the first part of this chapter. Skovsmose (2011) has recently attempted to review his conception of critical mathematics education. However, in the acknowledgements to the book he admits that this is not a possible task. Rather than a concept that can be described simply by reference to a theoretical basis and be evidenced in classroom practices, he sees critical mathematics education as a preoccupation which engages us in discussions and debate about the nature of the social and political context in which we work, and the ways in which our students experience mathematics and mathematics teaching and how they make connections between their learning of mathematics and the situations in which they live their lives. He also sees exploration of the ways in which learning of mathematics takes place outside the formal classroom, and the ways in which mathematics impacts on our everyday lives, as central to the 'preoccupation' of critical mathematics education. These ideas were discussed in more detail in Chapter 1 and relate to the formatting power of mathematics. Perhaps most importantly, Skovsmose sees reflection at the centre of critical mathematics education. This includes reflecting on our own 'foregrounds'; that is, how we bring our previous experiences of current social and political context to bear on the teaching and learning of mathematics. This links to the notion of identity discussed in the next two sections. The research reported below engaged both students and teachers in reflecting on their relationship with the teaching and learning of mathematics.

Mathematics learning and identity

In many countries, teaching has become defined by sets of 'standards' or 'performance indicators' which are used as a form of curriculum for teacher education programmes of performance management indicators used to 'assess' teacher performance. These 'standards' have become embedded in classroom practice and have led, in some cases, to a 'common sense' view of teaching and learning mathematics which students in our schools may come to accept as 'good' practice.

These trends were exemplified by two groups of students I worked with to explore their personal views of learning mathematics and of themselves as students of mathematics (Cotton 2008). One group were 11 years old and had just started at an 11–16 secondary school in the UK, the second group were just coming to the end of their time at the same school and were defined by their teachers as 'disengaged' from learning mathematics.

I asked both groups to draw a mind map that described, for them, what it was to be 'good at maths'. The younger group treated this is as a collaborative activity, engaging in discussion before making their mind maps. The posters all used an imaginary figure or a figure from history to characterise someone who was successful in mathematics. The figures from history were scientists such as Thomas Edison, and the 'imaginary' figures contained the stereotypes which have appeared in previous studies of this type. When the students described what skills these people had they listed: they do not need to use calculators; they can answer questions very quickly; they can use all the mathematical operations well; they use complex mathematical vocabulary and explain things well. This suggests that the group has a fairly narrow view of the nature of mathematics that is limited to arithmetic. They also seem to see 'being good at mathematics' as something out of the 'norm'. In other words, the 'mad scientist' or 'geek' stereotype persists. However, at the same time they could all describe peers who they saw as good mathematicians, and several pointed out individuals within the group. One whispered to me that they knew one of their friends was good at maths because the teacher always asked them the questions, this was seen as positive as she said, 'It's great, we always let them answer the questions so we can get on quickly.'

In contrast, the older students did not cite any peers as examples of people who are 'good at maths'. All of these students used their current teacher as a model for someone who is good at mathematics. They described success in mathematics as mastery over content. A summary of their discussion is that individuals who are 'good' at maths understand the content and that these individuals are also 'boring'. This view of successful learners in maths was in direct contrast to their view of themselves as students and they could not see any way that their identities as individuals were compatible with an identity which would include being successful learners of mathematics. More worryingly, such a view was beginning to emerge with the younger group of students too.

To further explore the young people's images of learning mathematics and their images of themselves as learners of mathematics, I asked them to draw images of 'what learning maths was like'. As in the previous activities, the younger students drew a wide range of images and articulated clearly how these images related to their prior experiences of learning mathematics; they could also describe their relationship to the images. However, the older students could not articulate what it was like for them to learn mathematics, and none of them could relate a time when they had felt successful in learning mathematics. One student commented that the activities they had worked on together during my first visit allowed them access to learning mathematics for the first time. In order to try to get the older students to engage with the question 'what is it like for you to learn maths?' I used the images that the younger students had drawn and asked them to sort them into two piles; those that resonated with their own ideas of what it was to learn mathematics and those that did not. This activity allowed them to begin to describe their feelings towards learning mathematics.

I then used a similar process with the younger group; they sorted the set of their own 24 images into two groups, and then selected a key image from the group that they thought fitted their view of the process of learning mathematics. They then explained in some detail why they had selected this image. For the 11-year-old pupils the key image was of a tape recorder sitting on a teacher's desk. There is no sign of a teacher. Lines emanating from the tape recorder make it clear that the tape recorder is controlling the lesson. There is also a sheet of paper resting on another desk. This is a pupil's answer sheet for a mental maths test. The pupil has written next to the image 'I like doing Mental Maths with the tape recorder in the Primary School'. This image refers to a process which, at the time of the research, was used by the national tests at age 11 in the UK. Pupils were asked to respond to a series of questions using mental methods. The process was standardised nationally by using a common set of questions delivered to schools on an audio-tape.

This image was selected by all the 11-year-old students as being an image that they saw as representative of 'what it was like to learn maths'. When I asked them to talk more about this choice they said, 'It's good because it says it clearly. The teachers take too long but the tape goes really quickly. Sometimes the teachers repeat themselves and it takes ages'. This suggests a view of learning mathematics as disembodied, literally in this case. The tape recorder was not required to take account of individual needs, it did not bring emotion into the equation. This view linked directly to the sense the young students had, that success in mathematics is measured through successful completion of tasks. This view cuts directly across the engaged view of teaching and learning mathematics that is offered by the authors of this book.

The older students selected three cards: one showed a pupil sitting at a desk, almost swamped by a huge piece of paper saying 'Oh no not maths again'; another image showed a face with swimming eyes with the statement 'learning maths is sometimes confusing'; their final choice was a card showing a sleeping pupil sitting at a desk with a teacher. The teacher's speech bubble contains 'Blah, blah, blah, blah, blah …'. The student has written on the card 'I don't like it when teachers take FOREVER to explain something and Boring [sic] teachers shouldn't teach maths'. When we discussed these choices further, the students told me that they felt teachers took too long to explain things, for these students the explanations were not supporting their learning, they said: 'It just makes me confused'; 'People get scared when they do their work because sometimes they can't solve it'; 'When I'm doing my maths revision at home it makes me mad and it makes me confused'.

This suggested an image of learning mathematics as a process of confusion and frustration, which could not be alleviated by the teacher trying to explain concepts and ideas. In fact, the lengthy explanations were perceived as increasing the frustration. Mathematics for these students appeared to be confusing, frightening and enraging. Again, this is something which does not fit with the view of mathematics being offered by this book. We should not be surprised by this; education in the United Kingdom and mathematics education in particular has not developed within a broad government view that a prime purpose of education is to ensure the sustainability of the planet and to develop social justice and human rights. Rather, the rhetoric around which education policy and practice is formed is that of supporting the growth of the economy and ensuring our 'competitiveness' with other countries.

The research with these students of mathematics revealed two distinct attachments. The group, at age 11, are able to see 'mathematics learner' as a facet of their identity. In contrast, the group of 16-year-old students, who were identified as 'disaffected' by the school, made no connection at all between their images of themselves and images of successful learners of mathematics. This disconnection makes any form of teacher–student relationship in the mathematics classroom very difficult. There was also a marked difference between the ways that the younger students could articulate their images of themselves, particularly in relation to school, learning and mathematics learning, and the older students who could articulate self-identity but often saw it in tension with what it is to be a learner of mathematics. These students found it very difficult to articulate their relationship to mathematics and mathematics learning, except as an opposition.

Mathematical subject knowledge and teacher identity

The discussion of teacher subject knowledge and pedagogical practice was developed by Lee Shulman in 1986 with the introduction of his idea of pedagogical content knowledge. Shulman suggested that teachers draw on three forms of knowledge in order to teach effectively. The first is a 'deep' knowledge of the subject itself; second, teachers need an understanding of the curriculum they are expected to teach; and third, they must be able to draw on an understanding of the range of pedagogical choices that are open to them which may support students in coming to an understanding of the content. This has been taken up widely within the mathematics education community as a model of subject knowledge on which teacher education and professional development courses can be built. This model suggests that in order to explore the ways in which 'subject knowledge' interacts with teachers' views of themselves as teachers of mathematics and in turn how this impacts on the pedagogical choices they make, we must view subject knowledge as comprising three parts:

1. *Subject matter knowledge (SMK):* This can be described as the extent to which teachers see themselves as having a 'deep' understanding of key mathematical concepts. In Richard Skemp's terms (Skemp 1977) they have a relational understanding of mathematics rather than an instrumental understanding. That is, they can move beyond a mechanical or rote view of mathematical processes to see the links and connections between the different areas of mathematics.

2. *Curricular knowledge (CK):* This can be seen as the extent to which the teachers are able to articulate the demands of the curriculum framework within which they are expected to work. This curricular knowledge also encompasses cultural expectations built into classroom practices. These expectations become evident when teachers interpret choices they are making as 'high risk' or cutting across what they perceive as 'classroom norms'. Andrew Harris (2006) describes

curricular knowledge as 'grounded in and constrained by, classroom experience values and beliefs' (p. 31).

3. *Pedagogical content knowledge (PCK):* For Shulman, PCK is described as, '[t]he most powerful analogies, illustrations, examples, explanations and demonstrations – in a word the ways of representing the subject which makes it comprehensible to others' (Shulman 1986: 9). For teachers of mathematics, this would include the examples they choose to introduce a particular concept, the particular pedagogical approaches they use, the ways in which they group their students, the way in which they structure their instructions and teaching. In particular it is an awareness of the choices that they make and why they make those particular choices.

A research project (Cotton 2010) explored the intersections of these forms of subject knowledge and the ways in which the triplet combines and separates, to influence our views of ourselves as mathematicians and mathematics teachers and the impact this has on our teaching.

The struggle to define ourselves as teachers of mathematics with 'good' subject knowledge can cause professional tensions if we are also exploring ways in which we can develop as teachers of mathematics 'as if the planet matters'. This is particularly difficult if we do not have models on which we can build. Most teachers certainly will not find the practices outlined in this book in 'standards' against which they are measured; they may not have observed colleagues exemplifying any similar practices and may not have been introduced to such ideas as part of their teacher education.

I worked with a group of beginning teachers from the UK, to explore their views of themselves in relation to teaching and to mathematics. These beginning teachers (in the last year of a four-year training course) all had clear images of what they describe as their 'best teacher'. This is a person who inspired them as a student and who they wish to emulate in their own careers. They could describe with clarity how this teacher operated, in a sense this is a vision to live up to. We could see this as an 'heroic other'. There is an amalgam of practices and beliefs which they have been exposed to both as a student in school, and as a beginning teacher. These are activities they have observed in school, or been exposed to in a university which resonate with their understanding of best practice. This set of practices is often embodied by teachers and described as 'good practice', these are ideas they want to try. We could see this as an 'iconic other'. Finally there is a set of 'standards' against which teachers know they will be assessed and inspected. We could describe this as the 'standard other'. It is against these 'mirrors' that the beginning teachers construct their identities.

Morwenna Griffiths (1995) describes 'self-identity' as a web. For these teachers, this web is made up of everything they bring to the classroom together with their sense of how they see themselves reflected in the mirrors described above. For Griffiths, the construction of identity is 'partly under guidance from the self, though not in its control' (1995: 93). Individuals only exist within the communities of which they feel they are members, and individuals exist differently within different communities. Identity here is slippery and cannot be pinned down. It can, however, be explored. Tony Brown and his colleagues (Brown *et al.* 2004) describe identity in a similar way. They suggest identity is not something we should attribute to individuals, rather identity is something that people '[u]se to justify, explain and make sense of themselves in relation to other people, and to the contexts in which they operate' (2004: 167).

Throughout the research project, I spent time engaging the beginning teachers in working at mathematics. In actively questioning and reflecting on their learning they were able to change the nature of their own subject knowledge, in terms of their beliefs about what it is to be a mathematician. In their own classrooms, they were then introducing their students to a form of mathematics that they had recently experienced themselves as students. This allowed them to be both tentative in terms of the possible outcomes whilst being secure in the process. They knew, or they trusted, that interesting things would happen. They were also moving towards a belief that mathematics is about questioning, exploring and justification and so these were elements that they inserted into their classrooms. This is the beginning of a 'preoccupation' with critical mathematics education.

It also appeared that the beginning teachers were making clear pedagogical choices that did not always fit with everyday classroom practices. They tended to prioritise ways of working which allowed them to develop caring and respectful relationships with their students. As new teachers, with groups of children they had only recently met, their first priority was to develop and sustain these relationships. A belief that lay behind any conviction about ways of teaching mathematics was that an effective teacher supports their students emotionally and socially.

However, although these beginning teachers drew on ideas and strategies that had been presented to them as good practice, this 'iconic other' had subsumed the 'heroic other' in that neither described teachers they were currently working with as models for their current practice. It seemed that the 'best teacher' that may have inspired them to become teachers had faded into the background during the four years of their training course. However, the overwhelming issue for all the beginning teachers, in terms of their identity as a teacher, was the 'standard other'. Many of the trainees described how they felt that they had to take on the mantle of the class teacher in order to be successful. This led to tensions as sometimes they 'could not be themselves'. One beginning teacher, who was still working in the class of a mentor in school, suggested, 'I don't really know what sort of a teacher I really want to be yet, I suppose I will be able to be myself when I have my own class.' She described this tension in another way, saying, 'I guess you just go with the style of the teacher you are with, I will move into my own style next year.'

Developing an ethos of reflection and critique in the mathematics classroom

In both projects, described above, the process of research allowed participants to begin the process of developing a vocabulary of critique about the context in which they found themselves. If we can describe what it is like for us to be in a particular situation, we can begin to think through the possibilities for change. The young students I worked with were coming to see the world through positivistic lenses. They could describe the characteristics of effective learners of mathematics, they seemed certain that people with these characteristics would succeed. Unfortunately, they described themselves in opposition to these characteristics and their positivist view of identity meant that they became excluded from this world. Exploring identity with these young people offered them a glimpse of a more complex world in which identities slip and slide and are not fixed oppositions. This gives previously excluded students room for manoeuvre, it opens up the possibility for them to find matches between facets of self-identity and their perceptions of what it is to be 'good at maths'. Such identity work, both with teachers and students, is an important part of any approach to critical mathematics education.

Reflection and critique of learning and teaching is at the core of what we are trying to present in this book; but we also argue that the 'content' of the curriculum should engage students in exploring issues that are of importance to them and at the heart of teaching as if the planet matters. In *Towards a Philosophy of Critical Mathematics Education* (Skovsmose 1994), Skovsmose offers four exemplars of the ways in which a thematic approach to teaching mathematics can support critical mathematics education. These exemplars offer models for 'projects' that we could develop in our own classrooms to support the development of critical mathematics education. The process of setting up such a project is as important to the agenda of critical mathematics as the 'content' of the project. Skovsmose had a research team who worked with teachers to develop these projects. Prior to working with the teachers, the research team talked to the staff in the school to ensure that any mathematical project would be building on interests and activities that were of relevance to the students and teachers. The students were also interviewed by the project team, to allow the researchers to begin to reflect on the students' 'foregrounds' and relationships to learning mathematics. Four projects are briefly described below.

Golfparken and constructions

'Golfparken' was a piece of land near to the school and the pupils were asked to work together to create, plan and design a new use for this piece of land. This involved the building of scale models, data collection from the local community to ascertain their views and visits by local advisors and experts to support them in coming to conclusions. This project led into 'constructions' which supported the pupils in building skills of construction and design. Here the teaching of mathematical skills came as a result of exploring a local issue using mathematics.

Family support in a micro-society

This project again resulted from some previous work which had led to pupils asking questions about child benefit. There are links here between this project and the ideas presented in Chapter 3. For this 'project' the class of 14/15-year-olds were asked to create 24 fictitious families and were then given the amount of money which would be available to these families in benefits to distribute between the families. As Skovsmose suggests in the book this was not a simple task. He says:

The more principal aspects of the formatting power of mathematics were touched upon by comparing the distribution of family support with other sorts of social regulations in which the conflict between what is possible to manage and what is reasonable and fair can be observed.

(Skovsmose 1994: 128)

Our community

This project grew out of a 'heated political discussion' amongst a group of pupils. There were concerns amongst the pupils about the provision of a range of services in their local community. The project was linked with a work experience programme for which the pupils had to apply formally and be interviewed. Then as a result of their experiences in a range of roles and through interviews with local politicians and community leaders, groups of pupils presented their solutions to the problems they had identified to groups within the community.

Energy

The final exemplar asked pupils to explore three issues related to energy: energy and food, farming, and electricity. The types of problems that the pupils were asked to engage with included: how much energy is stored in certain food and how much is expended in particular tasks; how much energy is needed to produce food and how much electricity is used in pupils' homes. This final question engaged the pupils directly in thinking about reducing energy consumption.

These four exemplars offer ways forward for those of us that share a 'preoccupation' with critical mathematics education or who are committed to teaching mathematics as if the planet matters. The approach in each case is similar; the 'content' grows out of class discussions about issues of social or political interest to students and teachers. There is a process of reflection throughout the activity both on the nature of mathematics and its learning and on the conclusions that are arising from the mathematics. Finally, there is often a presentation of the results or conclusions both to fellow students and to those from outside the classroom who have been involved in the process.

The first part of this book used broad social and political ideas as starting points for the mathematics. There is a shift in the second half and in the chapters that follow; we start with ideas and concepts from mathematics and explore how these can be developed within the context of a critical approach.

There are similarities between what follows and a curriculum development project undertaken for Nottingham City Council, UK (2010) focused on developing and integrating global and anti-racist perspectives within both the primary and secondary mathematics curriculum (the same project that was discussed in Chapter 6). The aims of that project were to use the teaching and learning of mathematics to meet the following requirements of an anti-racist educational process:

- develop learners' understandings of cultures other than their own;
- enable learners to reflect on and develop positive attitudes towards cultural and linguistic diversity;
- use resources which draw on learners' cultural heritage and experience and which counter or challenge bias;
- use familiar contexts as starting points;
- illustrate the diverse cultural heritage of mathematics;
- critique and challenge stereotypical views of particular groups of people through the analysis of data;
- encourage collaborative learning.

The anti-racist process was supported by offering teachers a planning pro forma, to bring the ideas above into preparing lessons. The pro-forma is reproduced in Table 7.1, as many of the prompts are relevant to the considerations of this book.

In the following chapters then, we focus on the areas of handling data, algebra, number, geometry and probability, using these areas as a mathematical starting point to explore how we can teach specific mathematical content 'as if the planet matters'. This is to support teachers who have the content of their teaching defined but who still wish to take issues of sustainability and human rights seriously. We have drawn on the questions in Table 7.1, in offering ideas for classroom activities.

References

Brown, T., Jones, L. and Bibby, B. (2004) Identifying with mathematics in initial teacher training, in M. Walshaw (ed.) *Mathematics education within the postmodern*, Greenwich, CT: Information Age Publishing.

Cotton, T. (2008) 'What is it really like?' Developing the use of participant voice in mathematics education research, in T. Brown (ed.) *The psychology of mathematics education: a psychoanalytic displacement*, Rotterdam: Sense Publishers.

Cotton, T. (2010) Diamonds in a skull: unpacking pedagogy with beginning teachers, in M. Walshaw (ed.) *Unpacking pedagogy: new perspectives for mathematics classrooms*, Greenwich, USA: Information Age Publishing.

Griffiths, M. (1995) *Feminisms and the self: the web of identity*, London: Routledge.

Giroux, H. (1989) *Schooling for democracy: critical pedagogy in the modern age*, London: Routledge.

Harris, A. (2006) Observing subject knowledge in action: characteristics of lesson observation feedback given to trainees, *Proceedings of the British Society for Learning in Mathematics*, 26(2), June, 31–36.

Nottingham City Council (2010) *GARP: Integrating Global and Anti-Racist Perspectives within the curriculum*, Nottingham: Nottingham City Council.

Shulman, L. (1986) Those who understand: knowledge growth in teaching, *Educational Researcher*, 15(2): 4–14.

Skemp, R. (1977) Relational understanding and instrumental understanding, *Mathematics Teaching*, 77: 20–6.

Skovsmose, O. (1994) *Towards a philosophy of critical mathematics education*, Dordrecht: Kluwer.

Skovsmose, O. (2011) *An invitation to critical mathematics education*, Rotterdam: Sense Publishers.

Table 7.1 Lesson planning prompts

Context of lesson	What is the background of the learners and how have you taken account of this in the planning? What is the learners' previous experience which has a bearing on their learning in this lesson?
Grouping of learners	What will be the most appropriate way of grouping pupils to develop collaborative approaches to learning?
Resources	To what extent do the resources I am using: • Draw on learners' own cultural heritage? • Counter bias in materials and teaching styles? • Draw on learners' own experiences?
Language	To what extent does the lesson: • Reflect cultural and linguistic diversity? • Develop learners' confidence in using mathematical language? • Develop positive attitudes towards linguistic diversity?
Mathematics	To what extent does the mathematical content of the lesson: • Offer challenge to the learners? • Present positive images of learners as mathematicians? • Use familiar contexts as starting points?
Collaborative learning	To what extent does the lesson: • Encourage learners to express and examine their own views? • Encourage learners to become involved in their own learning? • Encourage learners to pose their own problems?

CHAPTER

Starting from handling data

Tony Cotton

Introduction

Several years ago, I carried out some work with a group of 10- and 11-year-old students in a school in Leicester. The class I was working with included students from a wide variety of backgrounds. The school was committed to a curriculum which both reflected the diverse backgrounds of the students and which worked for a more socially just society, both within and without the school. In fact, for the first two weeks of every year the whole school explored the theme of 'Respect', using a totally cross-curricular approach to learning and teaching during that time. In working for social justice in this way, the school had adapted its curriculum to take account of teaching 'as if the planet matters'.

For the six weeks that I was working in the school I had been asked, by the class teacher, to 'cover' the data-handling content within the scheme of work that the teacher had been following. I was particularly interested in the group posing their own problems and using their own mathematical skills to come up with solutions. I asked the class what they were interested in finding out about, or changing, in terms of their experience in school. The class agreed that they should look at different ways of arranging the classroom, explore how satisfied students and their teachers were with school dinners, and explore attitudes towards race and racism. (Of course, coming to this agreement was an exercise in data handling itself.) The students then selected which group they wished to join.

The group focusing on race and racism designed a questionnaire. They decided who they would use this questionnaire with and then analysed the responses and reported back to the class. They reported back using bar charts, line graphs and pie charts with each group describing why they had chosen particular representations to illustrate their data. Some of their results are given below:

How would you feel if someone made fun of your skin colour?
- I would hit them   16%
- I would be sad   34%
- I would be angry   38%
- I would think they were ignorant   12%

What would you do if no one would let you play because you looked different to them?
- I would ask them why   42%
- I would let a teacher know   58%

Two people wrote 'I would be sad and play with someone else' and another wrote 'I would wish I could change my skin colour'.

If you were on a bus and you had a spare place next to you how would you feel if there were lots of people standing and no one would sit next to you?
- I would think they didn't like me because I am different   64%
- I would ignore it and be happy because I wasn't squashed   36%

This approach to handling data made direct links to the students' lived experience; it also allowed the teacher to bring mathematics directly into the personal, social and health education (PSHE) curriculum, which focused on these issues for the following three weeks. It opened the adults' eyes to issues they had not been aware of, the day-to-day prejudice impacted on students when they travel on public transport and the damage to self-esteem suffered when students are made to feel that 'they want to change their skin colour'.

I suggest that the students came to understand the mathematics of data handling more deeply from this project than they would have done from surveying something less meaningful, such as shoe sizes. They explored questions that they were committed to, and they had to decide how to 'tell the story' accurately with the data so that people could understand the issue.

Data handling

The data-handling cycle is often represented by a diagram similar to Figure 8.1.

The diagram illustrates the cyclical nature of any data-handling activity. It also emphasises the importance of posing a problem, or a question that students genuinely want to know the answer to. Perhaps more importantly, it suggests that any cycle of data handling and data interpretation will throw up new questions to be explored.

In Chapter 7, I used Giroux's definition of critical education. This suggested that 'schools ... [should] educate students to be critical citizens' who can think, challenge, take risks, and believe that their actions will make a difference to the larger society'

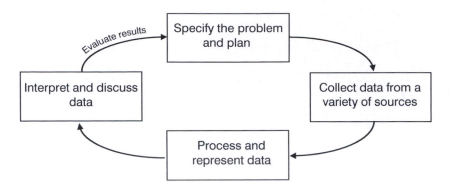

Figure 8.1   A data-handling cycle

(Giroux 1989: 214). I also suggested that a mathematics education could be constructed with the explicit aim to work towards developing citizens who could take their place in a democratic society rather than simply being seen as a tool for furthering economic aims of the country.

Drawing on this rationale for a critical approach to teaching and learning mathematics, this chapter shows how a shift to expecting students to engage in the data-handling cycle as a whole rather than view it as disparate parts allows them to become critical in the way they engage with the data. If we look at the data-handling cycle in more detail, and think explicitly about a critical approach to data handling we can describe it as follows:

1. *Specify the problem:* ask a question or questions. This in itself can be a democratic act. Many of the questions that students see as important relate to their lived experience.
2. *Plan:* decide what data to collect, who to collect it from and how to collect it. This is an important skill for all those who wish to make decisions based on the best available evidence. This is exactly the type of skill we would want to see in critically numerate citizens.
3. *Collect data:* gather the appropriate data from your primary or secondary source, as quickly and efficiently as possible. We also need to ensure that we collect data from a wide range of sources so that all points of view are taken into account. This is a key issue in any form of democracy.
4. *Process and represent:* reduce the raw data to summary information to help to answer your question(s). This summary information must be accessible to a range of audiences which demands that students are aware of a wide range of possibilities in terms of presenting the data.
5. *Interpret and discuss:* use the data to answer the initial question(s) and consider supplementary questions. This is how we can develop the skills of analysis and critique.

The following two tasks give examples of how this approach has been developed in the classroom.

Activity 1: If the world were a village

The book *If the world were a village* (Smith and Armstrong 2004) offers 12 sets of data which imagine the world were a village of 100 people and give the data as if it were represented by this data. Clearly, just another way of looking at the data in percentage form, but a neat way of allowing young students to make sense of large numbers.

The book explores data under the headings: nationalities; languages; ages; religions; food; air and water; schooling and literacy; money and possessions; electricity; the village in the past.

I will look at how it would be possible to develop activities drawing on two exemplars from the book. These are 'air and water' and 'money and possessions'. The book introduces the data as follows:

Air and water

When the book was written, there were more than 6.7 million people on the planet. Picturing this many people is difficult, so the book imagines the whole world as a village of 100 people.

In most of the village, the air is healthy and the water is clean. But not all the villagers are so fortunate. For some the air and water are soured by pollution, putting them at risk of diseases. Or water may be in short supply. Instead of turning on a tap, some villagers must walk long distances to find clean water.

Fresh air and drinkable water are necessities. How many people in the village of 100 have clean air and a nearby source of clean water?

82 have access to a source of safe water either in their homes or within a short distance. 18 must spend a large part of each day simply getting safe water. Most of the work collecting water is carried out by women and girls.

64 have access to adequate sanitation meaning public or household sewage disposal 36 do not.

68 breathe clean air.
32 breathe air that is unhealthy because of pollution.

Money and possessions

In one part of the village someone buys a new car. In another part a man repairs his bicycle, the family's most valued possession. How much money do the people in the Global Village have?

If all the money were divided equally, each person would have about £3,600 per year. But in the Global Village the money isn't divided equally.

The richest 20 people have more than £5,600 a year
The poorest 20 people have less than 65p per day
The other 60 people live on something in between

The average cost of food, shelter and other necessities in the village is £2,500 to £3,000 per year. Many people do not have enough to meet these basic needs.

Possibilities

The first activity that this data could be used for is to imagine the world as represented by the class you teach. So instead of looking at the data as represented by a percentage, adapt this for 32 students or however many are in your class. So, using the 'air and water' data, in a class of 32 students:

- 26 would have access to safe water; 6 would not
- 20 would have access to adequate sanitation, 12 would not
- 22 would breathe 'fresh' air, 10 would not

There are 10 sets of data, so this lends itself very well to splitting the class into groups of three or four, and letting each small group work on one of the data sets. Each small group can then divide the class up to be representative of the data they have been analysing. This activity works well if the class divide themselves up initially according to what they think the proportions will be.

This sort of activity can be carried out in a year assembly where students are all given 'colours' or other symbols and asked to group themselves in different parts of a hall. Another effective strategy is to not assign 'labels' to the groups but to offer the whole group the set of labels and ask them to try and predict which label should be attached to each group by examining the data.

A second possibility draws on the use of a drama technique called 'The Mantle of the Expert'. This was developed by Dorothy Heathcote (see, for example Heathcote and Bolton 1995) and forms the bedrock of much drama in education teaching. The 'Mantle of the Expert' website offers the following as a brief introduction:

> The Mantle of the Expert is a dramatic-inquiry based approach to teaching and learning invented and developed by Professor Dorothy Heathcote at the University of Newcastle upon Tyne in the 1980s. The aim is that the class do all their curriculum work as if they are an imagined group of experts.
>
> Because they behave 'as if they are experts', the students are working from a specific point of view as they explore their learning and this brings special responsibilities, language needs and social behaviours.
>
> (Mantle of the Expert.com n.d.)

For this second possibility, the mathematics class becomes a publishing company. The initial task is for the group to decide what different roles would need to be fulfilled by a publishing company. It is important that the class decide this as this ensures they will take responsibility for the company once the 'commission' is made. It is likely that they will decide on people with responsibility for text, for illustration, for marketing, for editorial control and so on. Once the class have agreed on these roles then the commission can be made. The commission is as follows:

The Association of Teachers of Mathematics have requested that the book *If the world were a village* be reprinted but with illustrations which offer mathematical representations of the data. They don't want simple pie charts or graphical representations but want imaginative and creative ways of illustrating the data.

The class would then need to decide how best they could meet this commission. The commission will involve them in representing the data in a range of ways. Members of each group will need to know how to illustrate the data, what text should accompany the illustration and carry out 'market research' to check that this new way of illustrating the data meets the brief. They will certainly need to research alternative ways of representing data. There are examples drawing on this data at www.toby-ng. com/graphic-design/the-world-of-100 and the students will be able to find lots more by exploring the web. The *New Internationalist* magazine also often uses a wide range of creative infographics to illustrate data.

Where this might go

A possible extension activity is to provide your class with relevant information which will allow them to compare local data with the international data you have been exploring. For example, even though it may be assumed that everyone within your area is accessing education, there will be data which details the number of young people who regularly do not attend school. The databases provided by the UK's Department for Education list all 'unauthorised absences' by school and by government region. In Leeds, for example, unauthorised absence ranges from 0.4 per cent to 6 per cent. Similarly there were 5,470 permanent exclusions in all schools during 2009–2010. This represents 0.08 percent of the school population. This is a reduction from 0.16 per cent in 1997/1998.

There will be data available of the ethnic background of the local population. The school could carry out a survey of the number of languages spoken within the school, or the religious backgrounds of the families within the school. As well as providing a useful mathematical activity, all of this data is useful for the management of the school to build a fuller picture of their students.

Another useful activity is to set about critiquing the data by drawing on alternative sources. Rather than simply accepting the data as it is presented in *If the world were a village* (Smith and Armstrong 2004), use the questions as the starting point for further data collection. So, for example, an assertion in the food section is that if all the food in the world were divided equally, then everyone would have enough to eat. This assertion could be used to set up a task in which the students draw on a wide range of data sources which they can research to explore the area of food resources (see Chapter 4). They may well all come up with different figures in terms of the proportion of the world's population who are 'well-fed', 'undernourished' and 'starving'. The differences in the data are important to acknowledge and to explore. It is this exploring of the different interpretations which will support your students in becoming 'critical'.

Finally, you can draw on other data linked to the millennium development goals to examine the progress made towards meeting these goals. If you log on to the millennium goals website there is a wealth of information. For example, one headline from 2011 was, 'Despite progress malaria kills one child every 45 seconds.' This headline could be the starting point for much critical mathematical activity. How many children will this be today? In this month? In the year? Where in the world is this most prevalent? If we were to reproduce this fact for particular countries what would the death rate (in seconds) be?

Activity 2: a sustainable school

This second case study is presented from a Nottinghamshire rural primary school who spent a day of their 'normal' timetable exploring issues of sustainability across the school. This had considerable impact both on the students and their teachers, which is described in detail in Watling and Cotton (2000). There were 48 students, aged 7 and 8, and two teachers engaged in the project.

This section outlines the process, which included the involvement of the local secondary school but also carries a 'health warning', the possible 'cost' in terms of simply 'dropping in' critical mathematics education activities to a curriculum which does not 'teach as if the planet matters' on a day-to-day basis. Both the students and the teachers found reverting back to their 'normal' curriculum frustrating. The students found it difficult to move away from the responsibility and 'power' that they had enjoyed in taking full responsibility for the curriculum and for the activities they had engaged in. Even after one day, they became much more questioning about the validity of the occasionally mundane activities that they were presented with in order to simply practise skills without any context. Similarly, the teachers felt much more hidebound by an imposed national curriculum which they felt they had to 'deliver' to their students without any control over the selection of the curriculum.

This is not an argument against engaging in critical mathematics activities but it is an acknowledgement that it is a challenge and that it is important to ensure you have allies in the form of curriculum development. It also shows that it is actually more difficult to carry out one-off activities which explore 'teaching as if the planet matters' rather than to reconfigure your whole way of working.

Possibilities

In preparation for the day, I worked with the drama group at the local secondary school to record a video in which they appeared as inhabitants from the Planet Zog who had heard that the adults on planet Earth were gradually destroying the Earth through careless use of the Earth's resources. The inhabitants of Zog set a challenge to the students from the school and asked them to send them a video that showed what they could do in their school to make it more sustainable. If this video convinced the inhabitants of Zog that the planet was in the safe hands of future generations they would call off their invasion of Earth. Whilst I was working in the secondary school, Rob Watling, a colleague, was setting up the project in the primary school. He talked to the two classes and told them that the 'Minister for Mathematics' was to visit the school next week to ask them to carry out an important piece of research for him.

On the day of the activities, I arrived in role as the Minister for Mathematics and played the video from 'Planet Zog'. Although several of the students recognised the 'aliens' as their brothers and sisters, they went along with the role play and enjoyed the 'pretence' as a way of setting up what they agreed was an important piece of research. The students then worked in groups to come up with a wide range of suggestions. The groups then prioritised the suggestions so that they were achievable within the timescale and could be entirely planned and delivered by the students. One group was assigned to make a video of the day which would be sent back to Planet Zog. The final list of projects was:

1. A traffic survey of vehicles passing the school on each of its boundaries in order to assess the environmental impact locally of vehicles.
2. Designing a poster for the village to raise awareness of environmental issues. This included designing and producing the poster, deciding where to site it and sticking within a budget of £5.
3. Designing a recycling paper bin to encourage recycling around the school. The group produced a scaled-down prototype of the recycling bin.
4. A survey of paper use around the school to calculate how much paper was currently used and how this use could be reduced.
5. A survey of ways that students travelled to school. The group surveyed the whole school and prepared a computer database of their findings as well as presenting the data in a range of ways for the video to be sent back to 'Zog'.

The finished video was sent to 'Zog' (in reality the local secondary) who prepared a response to the work of the students as another video We are pleased to say that the invasion of the Earth seems to be have been postponed.

Where this might go

Such a project, focusing on developing a more sustainable school, will both engage your students and allow you to engage in a wide range of problem solving activities. As with the group of students above, the most effective way to begin such a project is to ask them how they could explore this issue. Do some research for yourself first. How much waste paper is thrown away each day? How much does the school spend on paper and photocopying? What are the annual fuel bills? What are the implications for pollution for the ways that students travel to school? Some other areas, that have worked well in the past, for extended projects include the following.

- *Car parking*: What is the most effective way of redesigning the car park so that it uses a minimum of space and so that it can incorporate a bike shed to encourage cycling to school? This involves measurements of cars, the construction of scale models and trying out different arrangements for parking spaces. The issue of ensuring there are sufficient parking spaces for those needing accessible parking is also important.
- *Travel to school*: Survey the whole school to find out how teachers and students get to school. Students can then calculate the current carbon footprint of these

journeys. This has led to students exploring ways of lift sharing, of walking, buses, or cycling schemes where they meet up and cycle to school together. The mathematics involved also involves exploring shortest routes to school, and possible 'pick-up' points.

- *Recycling paper*: Again a brief survey can ascertain which classes use most paper; which classes are best at recycling paper and the money that can be saved through recycling paper internally as scrap paper, or in home-made exercise books. A trip to a recycling plant is always popular.
- *Energy bills:* Sharing the energy costs within a school has always led to students becoming incredibly vigilant about turning off lights and thinking carefully about energy usage. We know of school leadership teams who have offered the student council a share of any money saved through cutting energy costs; the student council has been able to make the decision about how they will spend this money.

Conclusion

Although the focus for this chapter has been data handling, it is impossible to remove data handling from other areas of mathematics. It would have made no sense to say to the young students who wished to design a recycling bin that they could not do this as we wanted to focus on data handling. It was data handling that allowed us to analyse the current situation and data handling that would allow us to see if there had been any impact, but it is vital that students see all areas of mathematics as connected rather than present the curriculum as distinct and piecemeal.

Similarly, it is important that the data handling we carry out explores questions that are of interest to the students we are working with. The environment and issues of sustainability are of great interest to the students in our schools. Our role as teachers, working to 'teach as if the planet matters', is to support them in developing the skills of data handling which will allow them to explore these issues rigorously and to come up with valid conclusions.

We also think it is important that the results of the research are shared. This can either be with other groups of students in the school, or preferably with people who can take action resulting from the students' findings. The outcomes of the questionnaire from the start of this chapter were presented at a meeting with the senior management team of the school and led to discussion of how the school's anti-racism policy should be adapted as a result of the findings. The head teacher of the school involved in the recycling project took up the suggestion of paper recycling bins and asked the group to survey the paper use in the school on a termly basis.

It is when data handling results in action and that action results in change that we see the true value of critical mathematics education. Students who can see change happening as a result of their research become more motivated to carry out similar research in the future and begin to see the power of critical mathematics.

Further reading

- *Bad science* by Ben Goldacre (2009) is a book to share with your older students as it exposes how statistics can be used to make mistaken observations about science. It is based on his *Guardian* column and is written in an entertaining and witty style.
- J. Michael Shaughnessy, Joan Garfield and Brian Greer (1996) contributed a chapter on data handling in an *International handbook of mathematics education*. This explores the historical role of data handling in mathematics curricula around the world and pays particular attention to the way in which ICT can support the learning and teaching of data handling.

References

Giroux, H. (1989) *Schooling for democracy: critical pedagogy in the modern age*, London: Routledge.

Goldacre, B. (2009) *Bad science.* London: Harper Perennial.

Heathcote, D. and Bolton, G. (1995) *Drama for learning: Dorothy Heathcote's Mantle of the Expert approach to education*, Portsmouth: Heinneman.

Mantle of the Expert.com (n.d.) What is moe? Available online at http://www.mantleoftheexpert. com/about-moe/introduction/what-is-moe/.

Shaughnessy, J. M., Garfield, J. and Greer, B. (1996) Data handling, in A. Bishop (ed.) *The international handbook of mathematics education,* Dordrecht: Kluwer.

Smith, D. and Armstrong, S. (2004) *If the world were a village: imagine 100 people live in a village,* London: A & C Black.

Watling, R. and Cotton, T. (2000) Critical reflection by correspondence: perspectives on a junior school 'media, mathematics and the environment' workshop, *Educational Action Research*, 8(3): 419–34.

Starting from algebra

Alf Coles

Introduction

This chapter sets out possibilities for work on algebra within the context of growth and decay. In Chapter 7, mathemacy was defined in the following terms, as being:

> a radical construct … rooted in the spirit of critique and the project of possibility that enables people to participate in the understanding and transformation of society.
>
> (Skovsmose 1994: 27)

The spirit of critique requires awareness. For example, we can take the statistics we are quoted in the media as truth, or we can be aware that there have been choices made in their collection, presentation and interpretation. The spirit of critique also requires an awareness of our own actions and the extent to which they may or may not contribute to the status quo. Within mathematics, Gattegno associates algebra with an awareness of 'dynamics' (1988: 77) or an awareness of process. For example, given a function $3\rightarrow4$, $4\rightarrow5$, $5\rightarrow6$, a student may be able to predict $6\rightarrow7$. It requires an extra awareness to be able to predict, e.g., $100\rightarrow101$. There is a need to become aware of what is happening to the numbers, as well as just being able to do it, a shift from 'it's going up in ones' to 'I am adding one to the number'. There is a need to become aware of the process, the dynamic, in order to notice a rule. The algebraic expression $n\rightarrow n+1$ is one way of capturing this awareness.

In Gattegno's sense of algebra, algebraic thinking becomes central to working mathematically (in any part of the curriculum). We are being algebraic whenever we step back from a process we are engaged in, to become aware of that process. The static representations of algebra 'hold' a dynamic process. Take, for example, $2x+2y$; it is a static representation, a single object, but it holds the processes of doubling and adding, for *any* two numbers. Part of the power of algebra comes from being able to interpret processes as objects and then perform processes on the processes (e.g., factorising).

Another definition of algebra comes from the work of Kieran (1996) who introduces three categories, which were used in a UK Royal Society/Joint Mathematical Council report (1997) into algebra:

- Generational activities which involve: generalising from arithmetic, generalising from patterns and sequences, generating symbolic expressions and equations which represent quantitative situations, generating expressions of the rules governing numerical relationships.
- Transformational activities which involve: manipulating and simplifying algebraic expressions to include collecting like terms, factorising, working with inverse operations, solving equations and inequalities with an emphasis on the notion of equations as independent 'objects' which could themselves be manipulated, working with the unknown, shifting between different representations of function, including tabular, graphical and symbolic.
- Global, meta-level activities which involve: awareness of mathematical structure, awareness of constraints of the problem situation, anticipation and working backwards, problem solving, explaining and justifying.

Gattegno's sense of algebra as an awareness of process or dynamics is clearly linked to this last category but is also perhaps present in the other two aspects. Generalising patterns requires a stepping back and awareness of the process of generating the pattern. Equally, shifting between algebraic representations or manipulating expressions (both transformational activities) can require the expression of a process in symbols (e.g., what happens to an expression when each term is multiplied by two).

From a critical mathematics perspective, if being algebraic is about a way of thinking, as seems to be implied by the definitions above, then it is part of the role of the teacher to support students in applying this way of thinking to contexts outside the classroom and mathematics. If becoming aware of what we are engaged in is a key to being algebraic, then being algebraic is actually part of the spirit of critique. Part of algebra teaching can be an explicit (meta-)commentary about this stepping back, this awareness of process, and the different spheres in which such a stance might be significant. As teachers, we can support students to recognise when they do this stepping back by recognising (ourselves) when we *observe* them being algebraic and making it explicit for them by commenting on what we have observed.

In the rest of this chapter, there are three tasks that support the development of different aspects of algebra, and these aspects are highlighted in parts of the write-ups. One task introduces an iterative approach to algebra and another one works with ideas of exponential growth. These are both areas of mathematics that are not always offered to students pre-16 and yet are arguably crucial areas for an understanding of environmental crises. Most of the methods that we currently work on in schools model situations that are predictable; increasingly we will be living in a world of uncertain events and, in the future, the school mathematics curriculum may need to include elements of iterative thinking that lead to chaotic dynamics and catastrophe theory (Kreith and Chakerian 1999).

Activity 1: Population decline and growth

Starting point

Human activity places a large number of species in danger of extinction. Chapter 5 set out some of the issues and mathematics behind biodiversity loss and the potential dangers this poses to human life. As well as measuring biodiversity it is crucial to be able to model and predict the size of the populations of individual species. You could display the data from Table 9.1 on a board.

If you were given this data in 1985, when would you expect tigers to become extinct in the wild?

Younger students will be able to do this from looking at the difference pattern, or drawing a graph. Older students can be encouraged to find an algebraic model.

Having made their predictions, you can provide the more up-to-date data (taken from the same source) in Table 9.2.

You may want to graph this data and consider why the graph did not continue in the expected pattern. How would you now predict the date when tigers will become extinct? If you wanted to expand this work beyond the standard mathematics curriculum, there would be scope for students to research some of the pressures on tiger populations and what is being done to try and preserve them (see, for example, the Arkive website n.d.).

Table 9.1 Tiger population 1970–1985

Date	Tiger population (thousands)
1970 (t=0)	37
1975 (t=5)	32
1980 (t=10)	27
1985 (t=15)	22

Source: http://wwf.panda.org/what_we_do/endangered_species/tigers/about_tigers/tiger_population/

Table 9.2 Tiger population 1990–2010

Date	Tiger population (thousands)
1990 (t=20)	12
1995 (t=25)	6
2000 (t=30)	5
2005 (t=35)	4
2010 (t=40)	3

Possibilities

Having looked at one species, students may be interested to work on a similar analysis of a different species. Data is available, for example, from the WWF Global website (n.d.). Students could also be encouraged to find out about the species they look at, for example from the Arkive website (n.d.). One species whose population is currently rising rapidly is, of course, humans. The risk to life from human over-population has been considered by some scientists to be the greatest threat we face (Ehrlich 1968), although this is a contested issue with claims about misuse of statistics (Kasun 1999). Whatever your perspective, assessing risks from population requires estimates of what the future population is likely to be and that in turn requires mathematical modelling. We can use historical data to make predictions for the future, as was touched on in Chapter 1 and this is one way a project could go.

Look at the data in Table 9.3, which contains historical estimates of global human population from 1750 to 1900.

Using this data, try to estimate the current global population, and the likely population in 2050. This could be done either by drawing a graph and extrapolating, by looking at difference patterns and/or by calculating an equation. You might want to call 1750 'year zero' for your model. (Do not read on if you want to do this yourself first!)

If x measures steps of 50 years from 1750 then, $P = 0.33x+0.64$; if x is in steps of one year you would need to divide the 0.33 by 50, hence, $P=0.0066x+0.64$.

You are likely to get a figure of around 2.37 billion as the population estimate for 2012. Students may want to ask a variety of questions at this point, if they are given the opportunity, e.g., how accurate is their estimate? What factors will have influenced population growth since 1900? Asking these kinds of questions introduces a meta-level of thinking *about* the use of algebra, linked to wider global issues (see Chapter 2 for links between population and economic growth).

An issue students may notice is that the data appears to be perfectly linear (i.e., in a straight line). It is worthwhile being suspicious of raw data that seems so perfectly to fit a mathematical model (a steady increase of 0.33 billion every 50 years) and, indeed, these data values were *chosen* (for the purposes of this book) all within the bounds of historical estimates, to make this model neat. You might want to see what other 'spin' it would be possible to put on the data, from taking other values within these bounds (Table 9.4).

Table 9.3 Historical estimates of global population

Year	Population estimate	Population (billions)
1750	640,000,000	0.64
1800	970,000,000	0.97
1850	1,300,000,000	1.30
1900	1,630,000,000	1.63

Source: U.S. Census Bureau

Table 9.4 Upper and lower bounds of population estimates

Year	Population lower bound (billions)	Population upper bound (billions)
1750	0.63	0.96
1800	0.81	1.13
1850	1.13	1.40
1900	1.55	1.76

Source: U.S. Census Bureau, http://www.census.gov/population/international/data/idb/worldhis.php

Stepping back (being algebraic) and choosing different values within these ranges, could you make it look as though population was increasing more rapidly than a straight line? Or more slowly? What estimates of current population (or by 2050) would your new data give? Who might be interested in suggesting different trends? A task for students could be to research on the web for other historical population data and try and find the most divergent estimates.

Where this might go

Students may or may not be aware that our current population is vastly more than 2.62 billion (a figure it exceeded in 1952). Table 9.5 contains estimates of global population for the last 100 years.

These figures could be graphed, along with figures from Table 9.3, to create a sense of the pattern of population growth. Based on this new data, what estimates would you now give for global population in 2050? What mathematical equations would it be possible to fit to this data? You could use a spreadsheet for this and the facility to add a trendline and display its equation. It is a complex task to fit an equation to this data without the aid of a computer, but a discussion is possible about the shape of the curve and what possible *type* of mathematical equation might fit the data (e.g., quadratic, exponential); the graph could then be extended by hand to create a new estimate for 2050.

How does this new estimate compare with the estimate based on data from Table 9.3? You might want to calculate the percentage error! How convinced are you by this new prediction? What factors will affect how the graph goes in the next 40 years? How good is the past as a predictor of the future?

It is possible to find data on the web that splits global population into regions (e.g., Gapminder, n.d.). It is evident from this data that the huge recent increases in population have come mainly from less-developed countries (e.g., India) and that developed (or 'over-developed') populations have remained largely stable in recent years (in some cases declining). This has led some commentators (e.g., George Monbiot 2008) to see concern about population as a way of blaming the poor, when in fact the greater threat to the planet is not over-population in less-developed nations but over-consumption in the developed ones. As was touched on earlier, the impact of population is a contested issue. For example, Alcott (2012) argues against playing one factor (over-population) off against another (over-consumption) and suggests, instead, developing the idea of a society's 'cultural carrying capacity' (p. 109) in determining

Table 9.5 Estimates of global population 1910–2010

Year	Population estimate	Population (billions)
1910	1,750,000,000	1.75
1920	1,860,000,000	1.86
1930	2,070,000,000	2.07
1940	2,300,000,000	2.30
1950	2,532,000,000	2.53
1960	3,038,000,000	3.04
1970	3,696,000,000	3.70
1980	4,450,000,000	4.45
1990	5,306,000,000	5.31
2000	6,122,000,000	6.12
2010	6,895,000,000	6.90

Source: www.geohive.com

each country's optimal population. However, there is no doubt that huge inequalities exist across the planet. In 1998, the United Nations provided some startling statistics around inequality in 1995 (figures for more recent years have not been calculated by the UN).

> Globally, the 20% of the world's people in the highest-income countries account for 86% of total private consumption expenditures – the poorest 20% a minuscule 1.3%. More specifically, the richest fifth:
>
> - Consume 45% of all meat and fish, the poorest fifth 5%
> - Consume 58% of total energy, the poorest fifth less than 4%
> - Have 74% of all telephone lines, the poorest fifth 1.5%
> - Consume 84% of all paper, the poorest fifth 1.1%
> - Own 87% of the world's vehicle fleet, the poorest fifth less than 1%
>
> Runaway growth in consumption in the past 50 years is putting strains on the environment never before seen.
>
> (United Nations Development Programme UNDP 1998: p. 2)

It would be possible to demonstrate these figures visually by splitting students into five equal groups and getting them to work out and then claim their proportion of, e.g., tins of tuna, light bulbs, paper from a pile in the centre of the room. Chapters 4 and 8 offer more ideas for activities linked to consumption and representing inequality.

Interlude

In fact, population models do not simply look at past data, but instead take into account (as mentioned in Chapter 1) fertility rates, life expectancy, death rates, birth rates, immigration, emigration in order to plot some possible future scenarios. These scenarios can then be assigned different likelihoods (see United Nations (2012) for the latest UN population predictions).

In a much simplified scenario, it is possible for students to engage in the kind of population modelling (not based on fitting an algebraic rule to a curve) that is a closer approximation to how mathematicians deal with the problem. It is accessible for students to work on deriving algebraic models for simple predator–prey relationships, which will entail useful work in interpreting and using algebra, potentially combining all three elements from the definition of algebraic thinking earlier in this chapter. Iterative algebraic thinking has been suggested as a key topic of a curriculum suitable for the third millennium (Kreith and Chakerian 1999).

Activity 2: Iterative population models

The models used in this task are based on differential equations. The presentation of ideas that follows has been done with 14–16-year-old students in mind, but it would be possible to use similar ideas with post-16 students, working directly with differential equations.

Starting point

There are many contexts in which population modeling is a vital task, for example, in order to assess the impact of human activity in a particular area. It has been suggested that errors in the modelling of fish populations were directly implicated in the over-fishing of stocks globally (Pauly 2007). Developing accurate models is therefore important for our survival as a species and it is possible to give students some insight into how such modelling is done whilst developing useful transformational algebraic skills and meta-level insights.

Imagine a population of animals living in a particular environment. The environment can only support a certain number of this species. If there are no major predators, how is this population likely to grow? Call the maximum population 1. Assume the population starts at 0.5, can you sketch a graph of how you think the population will grow? Can you find a function to generate the *next* population value?

It is likely that students will realise that as the population approaches its maximum value, it will increase at a slower rate. There will be decisions about how long to let students explore their own ideas. It is perhaps intuitive that the population will have some kind of growth rate over time (r). Students' initial ideas may be along the lines of $x_{n+1} = rx_n$ (perhaps not expressed in this way!) and it may be useful to see how this model either leads to runaway growth or the death of the whole population. To model the scenario presented, growth must be constrained somehow. In other words, $x_{n+1} = rx_n - ?$, where a function of x must be found that will stop this model predicting runaway growth (or decline). Students can try out their own ideas.

The way x has been set up (with a maximum of 1), it is effectively a proportion of the maximal population. Since it will be less than 1, squaring will make it smaller; the simplest model for this kind of population scenario uses a squared function as the 'restraint' on growth. Students may well come up with this idea, or other ones that can be explored. At some point you may want to introduce a standard model:

$$x_{n+1} = rx_n - rx_n^2$$
$$x_{n+1} = r\left(1 - x_n\right)x_n$$

The value of r is linked to the birth and death rate of the population, the bigger the value of r, the quicker the population grows, as can be seen from three scenarios in Table 9.6, all taking the starting proportion for x as 0.5:

Table 9.6 Three scenarios of population growth

r=0.5	r=1	r=3
0.5	0.5	0.5
0.125	0.25	0.75
0.05468...	0.1875	0.5625
0.02584...	0.15234...	0.73828...
0.01259...	0.12913...	0.57966...
0.00621...	0.11245...	0.73095...
0.00308...	0.09981...	0.58997...
0.00153...	0.08984...	0.72571...
0.00076...	0.08177...	0.59715...
0.00038...	0.07508...	0.72168...

In this model, r can vary between 0 and 4 (students can explore this – outside these bounds the population becomes negative!). One thing students could explore is the effect of r and therefore what it might be linked to in the real world. Using this model, students could explore (e.g., on a spreadsheet, and/or a graph) if the population reaches a steady state, for different values of r and different starting values of the population. Can you predict the steady state, given r? Can you prove your idea algebraically (e.g., setting $x_{n+1} = x_n$)?

Possibilities

In reality, there are only very few examples of populations living without predators. It is possible, however, to extend the model to deal with a simple predator–prey situation. This may begin to offer students a glimpse of the power of iterative thinking and modelling and also the complexity of behaviour that can result from relatively straightforward models.

If x models the number of prey, y can model the number of predators.

How is the population of x likely to change, given it now has y predators? How can we add this to our model?

A crude way to model the two populations is to imagine there are xy interactions between the species, in a given time period, and that these interactions are generally bad for prey and good for predators. So the model for x alters by having an extra term to deal with being eaten by predators. The value β captures how 'bad' each interaction is for the prey:

$$x_{n+1} = r\left(1-x_n\right)x_n - \beta x_n y_n$$

The final part of the model is to find an equivalent equation for y. In this case, although y is also a proportion, it does not have a *fixed* limiting value for its population (as we assumed for x), since if the number of prey increases, so does the maximum possible number of predators. To arrive at the model, we assume y will have a natural growth rate (s) in the absence of any prey (s will be less than 1, since with no prey, the population will dwindle). Then there needs to be a term linked to the number of interactions (xy) with the prey. The parameter, A, captures how 'good' each interaction is for the predators:

$$y_{n+1} = sy_n + Ax_n y_n$$

With these two models, students can explore population dynamics for different values of the parameters. A starting point, that gives a sense of how the model can work, would be to take $r=2, s=0.8, \beta=0.5$ and $A=1.5$ and initial values for x and y of 0.6 and 0.1 respectively.

Students may be able to generate values on a spreadsheet and plot x against y. The graph in Figure 9.1 resulted from the values above. Again, students can be invited to try out different parameter values and see if they can predict the limiting or steady state.

The parameters can be varied to explore different scenarios. For some values (such as the ones above), a stable balance is eventually achieved. In some cases, one of the

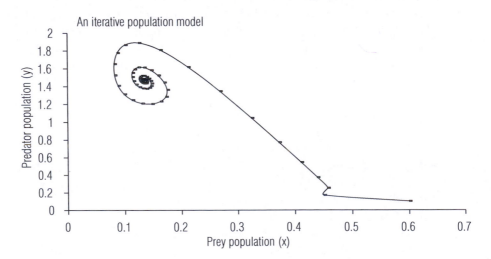

Figure 9.1 A graph of a predator–prey relationship

populations collapses and in other cases there may be oscillation between states. There are various web applets where this kind of relation can be explored. There is also open source software called StarLogo, developed by MIT, that allows an exploration of predator–prey and many other scenarios (see StarLogo (2008) for details).

Where this might go

Iteration is one way of solving equations often overlooked in school curricula. However, it can provide an opportunity and context to practise transformational algebraic skills that are often seen to be hard and with little purpose. It is also a way of validating what can be quite intuitive ways of students handling more complex equations.

For example, if we have an equation $5x - 4 = 2x + 8$, one way to go about solving it is to re-arrange to get x, leaving another x on the other side (which, intriguingly, is often what students want to do when they first meet this kind of equation). So, you might get:

$$5x = 2x + 12 \text{ and hence } x = \frac{2x + 12}{5}$$

To make this iterative, we can think of it as the method of generating the 'next' value of x; it is possible, but not necessary, to formalise this as: $x_{n+1} = \frac{2x_n + 12}{5}$.

If we 'run' this iterative equation, we will have found a solution if we find a value of x that maps onto itself and makes the original statement consistent. For example, starting with $x = 0$ on the right hand side, we get:

$$x = \frac{2 \times 0 + 12}{5} = 2.4$$

This is clearly not consistent (x is 0 on one side and 2.4 on the other) so we begin again with 2.4 as the value of x on the left hand side. After only a few iterations we find $x = 4$ is a value that maps to itself (a graphical calculator, or a spreadsheet can be set up to run this) and we have found a solution. Of course, in this instance, that solution could have been found more simply using a standard method. However, one of the powers of an iterative approach is that it can extend to quadratic and other kinds of equations. For example, to solve $x^2 - 5x + 2 = 0$ (which does not factorise), the quadratic can be re-arranged to:

$$x^2 = 5x - 2 \text{ and then } x = \frac{5x - 2}{x} \text{ or } x_{n+1} = \frac{5x_n - 2}{x_n}$$

A starting value of 0 will now be problematic, so take $x = 1$ and again the iteration quickly converges to 4.562 (to 3 decimal places). There are other possible re-arrangements, for example we could also use $x = \sqrt{5x - 2}$ and this would converge on the same solution; however, not all re-arrangements will work iteratively (this can be something to explore) and in the case of quadratics it may not always be possible to get the second solution, although usually by choosing different starting values this can be done.

Activity 3: Disease – exponential growth (with acknowledgment to Elizabeth Stewart for the original idea for this activity)

Starting point

Along with a rising human population, as a species, we are becoming more mobile than ever. This interconnectedness raises the potential risk of a catastrophic disease that could seriously impact human and/or other forms of life on the planet. The focus of this project is on modelling epidemics and giving students an experience of exponential growth. Mathematicians work on models of the likely spread of epidemics in order to calculate, for example, quantities of vaccination needed. You might want to begin the first activity without telling students what it is about. In the description below, the example is the spread of AIDS in South Africa, where around 15 per cent of the population are HIV+. You may want to choose a different country or epidemic.

Give all the students in your class a card. Mark 15 per cent of those cards with a black spot, tell the students this number but perhaps not the significance. Students must not show their cards to anyone else. Students get out of their seats and find a partner. They show their cards only to their partners. If one in the pair has a black spot, *both* people draw a black spot on their card (even if they have a spot already). Then give students time to move around again and find a partner (who can be the same person). As before, they compare cards and add black spots if necessary. Do this a third and possibly a fourth time.

Get students to guess how many of the class now have black spots. To find the number, get students to line up, those with four spots, three, two, one and zero.

Until you do this task yourself, you may be shocked at how quickly spots spread. Marking, say, five out of 30 cards, after four or even three iterations most students will have a black spot.

At this point you may want to raise a discussion of what the students think this has been about.

Having done this actively, students can then be invited to work on the algebra of this situation and set up a model to describe it and hence predict the spread of epidemics.

Possibilities

The simplest scenario is to imagine that everyone with a black spot infects someone new in each time period, so if there were four people infected at $t=0$, the number of infections (n) would proceed as follows: $t=1$, $n=8$; $t=2$, $n=16$; $t=3$, $n=32$, and so on. This is an easy pattern to describe but not necessarily to model. Students may well not have come across exponential models before, in this instance, $n=4\times 2^t$, where t is non-negative.

Refinements to the model can be made on the assumption that only a certain proportion of those infected at any one time will infect someone else by the next time. In the AIDS example this could be linked, for example, to condom use. If only 50 per cent of those infected infect others, starting from $n=4$ at $t=0$, in the next time period there will be six people infected, and at $t=2$, $n=9$; at $t=3$, $n=13.5$ (a decision will need to be made about rounding to integers or not!). Given one model, students may be able to adapt it to find other algebraic relationships, in this instance, $n = 4 \times \left(\dfrac{3}{2}\right)^{t}$. The

situation could also be modelled (perhaps for post-16 students) as an example of the binomial distribution, with each 'trial' offering a probability of infection.

Where this can go

The successive terms of the models above are essentially geometric progressions. In the case of AIDS, drugs are needed regularly in order to keep people healthy. Taking the simplest scenario possible, if each victim requires one prescription of drugs in each time period, then to find the number of prescriptions needed (for example, up to $t=10$) requires summing the terms of the sequence. Taking the example above, where everyone infects someone new each time period, if there are four people infected at time zero, there is a need for four prescriptions. At $t=1$, there are now eight people infected who will all need prescriptions, so by $t=1$ there would be a need for 12 prescriptions in total. There are methods for calculating the sum of a geometric progression that, although perhaps beyond the syllabus for 16-year-olds, can provide a motivation for useful transformational activity that would be on the syllabus. One method is given below, where S is the sum required, a is the number of initial infections and r is the 'multiplier' to get the number of new people infected in each time period.

$$S = a + ar + ar^{2} + ar^{3} + \ldots + ar^{n}$$

$$rS = ar + ar^{2} + ar^{3} + ar^{4} + \ldots + ar^{n+1}$$

$$S - rS = a - ar^{n+1}$$

$$S(1 - r) = a(1 - r^{n+1})$$

$$S = \frac{a(1 - r^{n+1})}{(1 - r)}$$

Students could be shown this proof and then asked to re-create it on their own.

Of course, there is also scope for students to look into the wider social consequences of the particular epidemic being studied. What is the role of the drug companies? How are drug prices set? How and where were drugs tested and trialled?

Further reading

- At the MIT website, there is an openware programme called StarLogo, based on the much older 'Logo'. With StarLogo you are able to control up to 50 'turtles' by defining rules for their interaction with each other and with the 'background' environment: http://education.mit.edu/starlogo/
- Up-to-date population information is available from the UN: http://esa.un.org/unpd/wpp/index.htm

References

Alcott, B. (2012) Population matters in ecological economics. *Ecological economics* 80, 109–20.

Arkive (n.d.) Tiger (*Panthera tigris*). Available online at http://www.arkive.org/tiger/panthera-tigris/ (accessed 2 March 2013).

Ehrlich, P. (1968) *The population bomb*, New York: Buccaneer Books.

Gapminder (n.d.) Gapminder world. Available online at http://www.gapminder.org/ (accessed 2 March 2013).

Gattegno, C. (1988) *The science of education. Part 2B: The awareness of mathematization*, New York: Educational Solutions Wordwide Inc.

Kasun, J. (1999) *The war against population: the economics and ideology of world population control*. San Francisco: Ignatius Press.

Kieran, C. (1996) The changing face of school algebra, Invited lecture presented at the 8th International Congress on Mathematics Education, Seville, Spain.

Kreith, K. and Chakerian, G. (1999) *Iterative algebra and dynamic modelling: a curriculum for the third millennium*, Boston: Birkhauser.

Monbiot, G. (2008) Population growth is a threat. But it pales against the greed of the rich, *The Guardian*, 29 January.

Pauly, D. (2007) Obituary: Ransom Aldrich Myers (1952–2007) Chronicler of declining fish populations, *Nature*, 447: 160.

Royal Society/JMC (1997) *Teaching and learning algebra pre-19*. Report of a Royal Society/Joint Mathematical Council Working Group. London: Royal Society, London.

Skovsmose, O. (1994) *Towards a philosophy of critical mathematics education*, Dordrecht: Kluwer.

StarLogo (2008) Welcome to StarLogo. Available online at http://education.mit.edu/starlogo/ (accessed 2 March 2013).

United Nations (2012) World population prospects, the 2010 revision. Available online at http://esa.un.org/unpd/wpp/index.htm (accessed 2 March 2013).

United Nations Development Programme (UNDP) (1998) *Human development report 1998*, New York: Oxford University Press.

WWF Global (n.d.) Priority and endangered species. Available online at http://wwf.panda.org/what_we_do/endangered_species/ (accessed 2 March 2013).

Starting from number

Jan Winter

Introduction

This chapter offers some starting points relating to number. There is inevitably quite a lot of overlap here with data handling activities since the focus is on using large numbers and often comparing numbers from data sets.

A key part of using mathematics as an informed citizen is to come to understand the implications of some of the data that is presented on a large, sometimes global, scale and how it affects individuals and their lives. This ability to deal with large numbers draws on basic number skills and applies them in a wide range of contexts and scales. This chapter presents some issues that could offer opportunities to experience the *reformational* power of mathematics, through critical analysis of the data. The issues also invite a *transformational* approach, going beyond critique of the outcomes (i.e. the data) to critique of the ways in which data can be arrived at and the choices implicit in them.

'Number' has often been seen as an unproblematic part of mathematics with few underlying values associated with its skills. This is far from the case. Choices are implicit in even simple calculations and these choices are associated with individuals' values. For example, the choices made in everyday purchases do not simply involve calculations following rules, they involve decisions based on personal choice and preference. In a supermarket it is generally the case that buying on a larger scale reduces the unit cost of items, a larger tube of toothpaste will usually cost less per gram than a smaller one. But does this mean that it is always 'better' to buy the larger item? If you are about to get on a flight carrying only hand luggage, then a tube of toothpaste larger than 100ml is not much use to you as you will not be allowed to take it on board. If you are buying a chocolate treat for your child then a 500g bar is not a good idea. What about 'BOGOF' (buy one get one free) offers? These seem too good

to miss, but if you cannot use the item (often fresh food) before its 'use by' date then it just encourages waste. Do 'buy two get one free' offers encourage over-consumption? And the cost of these offers is covered somewhere in a shop's pricing policies, so are we all paying the cost of such offers whether we buy them or not?

Numeracy has been defined in many different ways over the years, ranging from the ability to accurately apply the 'four rules', to being able to use a calculator efficiently, to having an 'at homeness' with numbers. A critical approach implies more than all of these, requiring students to question the basis on which calculations are made and the underlying implications of them. Barry Cooper and Mairead Dunne (2000), in work that focused on the use of 'realistic' items in mathematics assessments, noted the interpretations that children make of items in test papers and their attempts to make sense of them in relation to their understanding of the 'real world'. For example, in a question asking children to list all possible pairings for mixed doubles tennis matches from four girls' and four boys' names, some children were influenced by the names, wanting to make 'suitable' pairings rather than list all the possibilities. It is clear from Cooper and Dunne's work that students bring their own interpretations of meaning with them into mathematics classes, and that we need to work with them in ways which help them use the mathematics they learn in ways that make sense to them and that make sense in relation to the mathematical aims of the questions set.

Activity 1: Comparing data on incomes in different countries

This task will use data (for example, gross national income per capita database from World Bank) to consider differences in people's experiences across the world.

Table 10.1 gives the highest 20 countries and the lowest 20 countries, by per capita income in US dollars in 2010:

Starting points

Initially, discussion about this data will help students to become familiar with it. For example:

- Are there any entries we don't understand?
- Why might Afghanistan be placed where it is in the list? (Its figure does not seem to match its position)
- How might the positions of the countries with no figures (e.g. Bermuda or Qatar) have been decided?
- Where would we expect the UK to appear in this list? How might we estimate where the UK would be? Here is the UK entry: 31 United Kingdom 38,560. Is this what was expected?
- What does the data 'hide'? For example, in the UK, what do we think the range of incomes might be? Not everyone will have an income of $38,560. How might this average have been calculated?
- What does this extremely wide range of incomes tell us about the kinds of lives people live in different countries?

Table 10.1 Table showing 2010 per capita income (in US dollars) of the top and bottom 20 countries

Top 20 countries			
1	Monaco	*183,150*	a
2	Liechtenstein	*137,070*	a
3	Bermuda	..	a
4	Norway	85,340	
5	Luxembourg	79,630	
6	Qatar	..	a
7	Switzerland	70,030	
8	Cayman Islands	..	a
9	Isle of Man	..	a
10	Denmark	59,210	
11	Channel Islands	..	a
12	Kuwait	..	a
13	Sweden	50,000	
14	Netherlands	49,750	
15	San Marino	*50,400*	a
16	United States	47,240	
17	Finland	47,160	
18	Austria	46,690	
19	Faeroe Islands	..	a
20	Andorra	*41,750*	a

Bottom 20 countries			
194	Tanzania	530	
195	Rwanda	520	
196	Uganda	500	
197	Togo	490	
198	Nepal	480	
199	Central African Republic	470	
200	Zimbabwe	460	
201	Gambia, The	450	
202	Mozambique	440	
203	Madagascar	430	
205	Afghanistan	*290*	a
205	Guinea	400	
207	Ethiopia	390	
208	Niger	370	
209	Eritrea	340	
209	Sierra Leone	340	
211	Malawi	330	
213	Liberia	200	
214	Congo, Dem. Rep.	180	
215	Burundi	170	

Key: 'a' means data for 2010 was not available.
A figure in italics is data for 2009 or 2008. Some rankings are therefore approximate.
The whole data set is available at http://data.worldbank.org/data-catalog/ GNI per capita ranking.

- How reliable do we think this data is? What difficulties might there be in making it accurate?

Possibilities

Calculations can be done to compare data at opposite ends of the table.

Writing Monaco's and Burundi's incomes in standard form shows how much larger one is than the other:

Monaco: $183150 = 1.83 \times 10^5$ (to 3 significant figures)
Burundi: $170 = 1.7 \times 10^2$

So income in Monaco is more than 10^3 times that of Burundi, that is 1000 times as much.

Where might this go?

These ideas could develop into consideration of other data relating to international comparisons. For example, data can be found on such indices as spending on education, number of people per doctor, literacy rates, life expectancy or population density.

Activity 2: Waste and recycling

Waste – how much do we produce? How much of various resources do we use? How much waste is recycled? What do we do with the rest? This task looks at how much waste we produce in the UK and how much of it we recycle in various ways. It encourages students to ask questions about their own use of materials and how their community manages waste.

Starting points

This is an activity for small groups of students (about four is probably ideal) to work on together that will offer opportunities for collaborative learning. The set of statements in Figure 10.1 refer to the waste and recycling of a 'typical' family in the UK. Each piece of information is printed on a card and the cards are shared between the members of the group. The task is to identify the questions to be answered (there are two included on the cards) and then to use the information to solve them. The basic rule is that this must be done by talking about the information that each student has, rather than by 'pooling' all the cards. This helps ensure everyone in the group stays involved and has useful information to contribute.

The challenge here is to understand the information and identify what is important in helping to answer each question. Students will have to decide on what level of accuracy it is appropriate to work to so that answers will be reasonable. The task is also designed to encourage discussion and collaboration. (Solutions to the two questions are at the end of this activity section.)

Half of the weight of the family's plastic waste is bottles.	275 thousand tonnes of plastic are used to make bottles in the UK each year.
How many plastic bottles does the family use each week, on average?	The family also recycle garden waste.
Garden waste makes up half of the total weight of their recycled waste.	As well as plastic, newspapers, glass, aluminium and garden waste, the family recycle cardboard.
'Residual waste' means waste that is not recycled.	15 million plastic bottles are made each day in the UK.
There are about 65 million people in the UK.	Each glass jar or bottle weighs, on average, 300g.
Aluminium worth £36 million is thrown away each year.	How much of the family's recycling (in weight) is made up of cardboard?
There are four people in the family.	About one-fifth of the paper and card produced in the UK is used to make newspapers.
12.5 million tonnes of paper and cardboard are used each year.	40 per cent of household waste is recycled.
The family throws away 40kg of plastic each year.	Residual waste per person is 275kg per year.
The family uses about 10 glass jars and bottles each week.	The family recycles 90 per cent of the glass jars and bottles that they use.
The family recycles all the aluminium cans that they use.	The family recycle all the plastic bottles that they use, but their other plastic waste cannot be recycled.
The family recycles aluminium cans weighing 500g each week.	The family recycles all of their newspapers.

Figure 10.1   Waste and recycling activity cards

Possibilities

The next steps for students could be to design a similar group task, either based on the same topic or on others, according to what is appropriate in the class context. In creating their own tasks (again, in groups) they will be focused on what information is necessary, what is irrelevant to the questions asked and how to ensure wording is unambiguous.

The next section of this activity offers a range of data that could be used in tasks based on waste and recycling. Some of the data has been used in the set of statements given as the starting point above. As they start to plan a group task, students might need to research more data on the area they are focusing on.

The following data is from the website of the UK's Department for Environment, Food and Rural Affairs (Defra 2012):

- The UK produces 280 million tonnes of waste each year.
- Around 40 per cent of waste from households is currently recycled, as of 2011, compared to 11 per cent in 2000/01.
- The average residual waste per person has reduced by 76kg since 2006/07 to 275kg/person/year (Residual waste is the amount of waste that is not recycled.)
- 52 per cent of commercial and industrial waste was recycled or reused in England in 2009, compared to 42 per cent in 2002/3.
- 55 per cent of municipal waste generated in the UK is sent to landfill, compared to an EU-27 average of 40 per cent. (EU-27 means all 27 countries in the EU)
- According to RecycleNow, UK recycling saves more than 18 million tonnes of carbon dioxide a year, equivalent to taking five million cars off the road.
- UK produces approximately 7 million tonnes of food waste per year (5 million tonnes per year in England) and about 90 million tonnes animal slurry and manure (40–60 million tonnes in England) that could realistically be available for utilisation by anaerobic digestion (AD) technology. In England this could generate at least 3–5 TWh electricity per year by 2020 (a heat equivalent of 6–10TWh) (TWh means terawatt hours, 10^{12} watts of energy running for an hour)
- The UK water industry treats 66 per cent of sewage sludge by AD, generating in the region of 1TWh per year of electricity in 2010.
- The diversion of biodegradable wastes to AD can reduce greenhouse gas emissions from landfill. For example, capturing the biogas from one tonne of food waste will save between 0.5 and 1 tonne of CO_2 equivalent.

This information provides the opportunity to ask many questions. Here are some starting points to help students plan a task:

- If the population of the UK is 65 million, how much household waste does the population produce each year? Roughly what percentage is this of the total waste produced? How is the rest of the waste produced?
- If 55 per cent of household waste is sent to landfill (i.e. not recycled), how much is this?
- An old-style lightbulb uses 100 watts of energy. So it would run for 1 hour using 10^2 watt hours. How can we compare this to 1 TWh?

A collection of data that could promote further discussion and prompt questions is provided in the next section.

All of the following data is from the website of Recycling Guide (Recycling Guide 2012).

- 1 recycled tin can would save enough energy to power a television for 3 hours.
- 1 recycled glass bottle would save enough energy to power a computer for 25 minutes.
- 1 recycled plastic bottle would save enough energy to power a 60-watt light bulb for 3 hours.
- 70 per cent less energy is required to recycle paper compared with making it from raw materials.
- Up to 60 per cent of the rubbish that ends up in the dustbin could be recycled.
- The unreleased energy contained in the average dustbin each year could power a television for 5,000 hours.
- The largest lake in the UK could be filled with rubbish from the UK in 8 months.
- On average, 16 per cent of the money you spend on a product pays for the packaging, which ultimately ends up as rubbish.
- As much as 50 per cent of waste in the average dustbin could be composted.
- Up to 80 per cent of a vehicle can be recycled.
- 9 out of 10 people would recycle more if it were made easier.

Aluminium

- 24 million tonnes of aluminium is produced annually, 51,000 tonnes of which ends up as packaging in the UK.
- If all cans in the UK were recycled, we would need 14 million fewer dustbins.
- £36,000,000 worth of aluminium is thrown away each year.
- Aluminium cans can be recycled and ready to use in just 6 weeks.

Glass

- Each UK family uses an average of 500 glass bottles and jars annually.
- The largest glass furnace produces over 1 million glass bottles and jars per day.
- Glass is 100 per cent recyclable and can be used again and again.
- Glass that is thrown away and ends up in landfills will never decompose.

Paper

- Recycled paper produces 73 per cent less air pollution than if it was made from raw materials.
- 12.5 million tonnes of paper and cardboard are used annually in the UK.
- The average person in the UK gets through 38kg of newspapers per year.
- It takes 24 trees to make 1 ton of newspaper (1 ton is approximately 0.9 tonnes).

Plastic

- 275,000 tonnes of plastic are used each year in the UK, that's about 15 million bottles per day.

- Most families throw away about 40kg of plastic per year, which could be recycled.
- The use of plastic in Western Europe is growing about 4 per cent each year.
- Plastic can take up to 500 years to decompose.

Where might this go?

The activity could move on from this data to consider some more local data, perhaps about the school or local town. Students can gather data from their local council about waste and recycling figures. How does the local community compare with the national figures given here? Are they about the same or not? If not, why might this be?
    Here are some targets that were set by the Government:

- 25 per cent of household waste should be recycled or composted by 2005
- 30 per cent of household waste should be recycled or composted by 2010
- 33 per cent of household waste should be recycled or composted by 2015
- The recycling targets for individual local authorities is 30 per cent by 2005–2006

These targets were set in 2000 and according to the data already given, the rate achieved by 2010 was greater than the target. Students can look at what future changes there may be to rates and what targets they might suggest. There are further links to recycling in Activity 3, Chapter 11.

Answers to two questions in the activity from Figure 10.1

(Note that all answers are rounded to reflect the approximate nature of all the figures used. This is an important mathematical skill for students to develop.)

Plastic bottles

Plastic bottles used per week = approximately 8
275,000 tonnes of plastic are used to make bottles in the UK each year.
15 million plastic bottles are made each day.
So each bottle weighs approximately $\dfrac{275,000 \times 1,000,000}{15,000,000 \times 365} = 50g$
The family throws away 40kg of plastic per year and half of this is bottles.
So, the number of bottles used each year is approximately $\dfrac{20 \times 1000}{50} = 400$

So, the number of bottles used each week is approximately $\dfrac{400}{50} = 8$

Unrecycled waste

Amount of waste that is not newspaper, cans, glass, plastic or garden waste recycled per year = approximately 30kg. This is the total of cardboard recycled.
To find the amount of cardboard waste recycled each year, find the weight of all the named types of recycling and take this away from the total of recycled waste.

Total waste that is not recycled is $275 \times 4 = 1100$kg

40 per cent of waste is recycled, so total waste is approximately $\dfrac{1100 \times 100}{60}$kg $= 1835$kg

So, recycled waste is approximately $1835 - 1100 = 735$kg

Recycled waste is divided into six categories: garden waste, newspaper, cans, glass, plastic and cardboard.

Garden waste

Half of weight of all recycled waste is $\dfrac{735}{2}$kg $= 370$kg (to nearest 5)

Newspaper

12.5 million tonnes of paper and card are produced each year.

One-fifth is used to make newspaper, so this is approximately 2.5 million tonnes. There are about 65 million people in the UK, so this is about $\dfrac{2.5 \times 1000}{65}$kg $= 38$kg per person.

This is about $38 \times 4 = 150$ kg for the family.

They recycle all of this weight.

Cans

The family recycle 500g of cans each week.

This is approximately $\dfrac{500 \times 52}{1000} = 25$kg per year (rounded to nearest 5).

Glass

The family uses about $\dfrac{300 \times 10}{1000} = 3$kg of glass per week.

This is about $3 \times 52 = 156$ kg per year.

They recycle 90 per cent of this, which is about 90 per cent of $156 = 140$ kg.

Plastic

The family throws away about 40kg of plastic each year.

They can only recycle the bottles, which make one half of this weight.

So they recycle 20kg of plastic.

The total of the categories above $= 370 + 150 + 25 + 140 + 20 = 705$kg.

So, the total waste not falling into these categories $= 735 - 705 = 30$kg.

Activity 3: How much green space do we have around us?

This activity uses a large data set on land use in England. Other data sets are available covering other countries too. We hear frequently of the need to build more houses, as populations grow and household sizes shrink. But this need inevitably leads to conflict when communities object to building on 'greenfield' sites. Is there spare land to use within already developed areas? Or is it important for there to be open land within these areas anyway? The arguments are complex and subjective, but need to be underpinned by use of data on how land is used at the moment. The numbers are often complex and a key skill is to get to grips with what they tell us about the areas we live in.

Starting point

Download the database of land use in England from: http://data.gov.uk/dataset/land_use_statistics_generalised_land_use_database (accessed 9 Aug 2012).

Look at the data relating to an area of England. An example is given in Table 10.2, but it is probably most interesting to use the area you live in. The database divides land use up into ten categories: domestic buildings; non-domestic buildings; roads; paths; rail; domestic gardens; greenspace; water; other land uses (largely hardstanding); unclassified.

Table 10.2 shows the data for South Gloucestershire, an area on the edge of the city of Bristol. This data is taken from the 'OA' sheet of the database. (There are three datasets given and it could be a further activity to investigate the reasons for the differences between the datasets.)

It could be easier to compare the figures if they were given using standard form, so converting each statistic could be a good starting point. The total area of the chosen region is then 5.23×10^5, to three significant figures. Convert each of the other statistics to this format and then order them. What does this tell us about the type of area we are looking at? What has happened to the accuracy of the data through presenting them in this way? Is it still reasonable to compare them directly?

Table 10.2 Land use in South Gloucestershire, UK

Total area	522783.64
Domestic buildings	8039.79
Non-domestic buildings	4377.22
Roads	16074.53
Paths	980.57
Rail	867.5
Domestic gardens	29232.86
Greenspace	423601.98
Water	29045.59
Other land uses (largely hardstanding)	10535.39
Unclassified	28.20

These figures are presented in thousands of square metres, to 2 decimal places. This means they are accurate to the nearest 10m².

Source: http://data.gov.uk/dataset/land_use_statistics_generalised_land_use_database

Go back to the original data and look at it in terms of percentages. What percentage of the region falls into each category? Is this a better way to compare the figures than presenting them in standard form? What has been gained and what has been lost?

Ask questions about the data and use them to build up a picture of aspects of the region. For example:

- How much 'domestic garden' space is there compared to 'domestic buildings'? What does this tell us is the approximate average size of a garden in this region? (You'll also need to make an estimate of the size of a house to calculate this)
- Where is the 'water'? What does this figure tell us about the position of the region?
- How does the area of 'greenspace' compare with other uses of land? What does this tell us about the region?

Possibilities

Move on to look at the same data for other areas of England. Look at a range of different types of location, places within cities, very rural areas, coastal areas, etc, and use the data to show how different these regions are in the way they use land. The class could divide up the country in different ways to generate a display of data about land use. This could be done as a spreadsheet activity, with calculations being entered into additional columns.

Where might this go?

This dataset is only a quite broad division of land use into simple categories. The investigation could be taken much further to explore land use in different countries, looking at agricultural uses, looking at vegetation types, etc.

Activity 4: Stan's Cafe

There is a UK theatre company called Stan's Cafe. One of their pieces of work, 'Of all the people in all the world', uses grains of rice to represent people: one grain of rice represents one person and piles of rice are used to illustrate groups of people and statistical data. This presents a very graphic image showing us comparisons between groups. Watch a video of their show on their website: http://www.stanscafe.co.uk/project-of-all-the-people.html.

Starting point

A bag of rice is brought into the classroom to represent a chosen number of people. This could be the population of the city or town that the school is in. One gram of rice represents 60 people as there are approximately 60 grains per gram. So a town with a population of 60,000 would be represented by a bag of rice weighing 1kg.

This representation can be discussed and the amount of rice needed for different sizes of group can be found. How much rice would represent:

- the school?
- London?
- the whole of the UK?
- the whole of the world?

Watch one of the videos on the Stan's Cafe website to give students some idea of the scale of the piles of rice that would be created by some of the larger numbers. What would a pile look like that represented the whole population of the world?

Students can then be asked to research items of data that they would like to represent. While the imagery of grains of rice is powerful, it is also possible to change the unit of representation to other items that are available. Multilink cubes could be used, with each cube representing a number of people that is suitable for the statistic being represented. For example, students might want to show the numbers of people commuting into work in their area using different forms of transport. One cube could represent 100 people and then piles could represent those using cars, bicycles, train and walking.

A display can be made and photographed to create a display of the data collected. Students can also show the calculations they have used to determine the amount of rice or other unit they needed to display their chosen data.

Possibilities

This activity can be focused on whatever activities it links with in other parts of the curriculum. For example, if work is being done on, say, health issues in science, data could be collected on epidemics around the world. Or comparisons can be made between sizes of cities and the way they have grown throughout history.

The unit being represented can move away from people to consider use of resources, or manufactured goods, or any other physical feature. It is important, though, to remember the power of the link with the human population and the potential for students to identify with the data being represented through considering themselves as one grain of rice in the piles displayed. For this reason, in the show by Stan's Cafe, each visitor is given one grain of rice as they enter so that they have a direct link with the data.

Where might this go?

As described above, links can be made to almost any area of the curriculum. If the focus is to remain on sustainability issues, the teacher will need to support students in identifying relevant data. A collection of suitable source material would give students useful starting points and a discussion to focus students' questions would be valuable. Identifying two or three key areas within which to work, such as 'population', 'food production', 'transport' or 'industrialisation', would keep the work focused on relevant statistics.

If Stan's Cafe are performing their show locally, a visit would provide a powerful stimulus to the work and encourage a thoughtful approach to the issues underlying the data. Alternatively, a collaboration between mathematics and drama in school could be developed leading to students' own performance.

Further reading

- *A mathematician reads the newspaper* by John Allen Paulos looks closely at the use of numbers in newspaper articles and at the ways in which we may be persuaded by those with specific interests. Paulos believes we all need to be informed readers so that we can make our own judgments about the numbers that are presented to us. The book is presented in fairly short episodes, some of which would be accessible and interesting to students as well as teachers.
- *How bad are bananas?* by Mike Berners-Lee provides the carbon footprint of a huge range of items, from bananas to nuclear war via many fascinating and thought-provoking items. It helps the reader to think about the wide range of factors involved in carbon emissions – not as straightforward an idea as we might think.
- Stan's Cafe website (http://www.stanscafe.co.uk/project-of-all-the-people.html) provides videos and information about the way the show was designed. It is a stimulating set of ideas to provide starting points for data to tackle in a classroom activity.

References

Berners-Lee, M. (2010) *How bad are bananas?*. London: Profile Books.

Cooper, B. and Dunne, M. (2000) *Assessing children's mathematical knowledge: social class, sex and problem-solving*, Buckingham: Open University Press.

Defra (2012) Wastes and recycling. Available online at http://www.defra.gov.uk/environment/waste/ (accessed 7 Aug 2012).

Paulos, J. A. (1995) *A mathematician reads the newspaper*. London: Penguin.

Recycling Guide (2012) Recycling facts and figures. Available online at http://www.recycling-guide.org.uk/facts.html (accessed 8 Aug 2012).

Stan's Cafe (2012) Of all the people in all the world. Available online at : http://www.stanscafe.co.uk/project-of-all-the-people.html (accessed 8 Aug 2012).

Starting from geometry

Alf Coles and Laurinda Brown

Introduction

This chapter offers possibilities of using geometrical thinking to lead into issues of relevance for the planet. Before getting to these activities, it is pertinent to consider what is meant by geometrical thinking. Perhaps the most widely used characterisation of geometric thinking derives from the work of van Hiele (1986). There have been several versions of, and additions to, van Hiele's hierarchy of levels; the one below comes from a synthesis by Burgher and Shaughnessy (1986):

> *Level 0 (Visualisation).* The student reasons about basic geometric concepts, such as simple shapes, primarily by means of visual considerations of the concept as a whole without explicit regard to properties of its components.
> *Level 1 (Analysis).* The student reasons about basic geometric concepts by means of an informal analysis of component parts and attributes. Necessary properties of the concept are established.
> *Level 2 (Abstraction).* The student logically orders the properties of concepts, forms abstract definitions, and can distinguish between the necessity and sufficiency of a set of properties in determining a concept.
> *Level 3 (Deduction).* The student reasons formally within the context of a mathematical system, complete with undefined terms, axioms, an underlying logical system, definitions, and theorems.
> *Level 4 (Rigour).* The student can compare systems based on different axioms and can study various geometries in the absence of concrete models.
>
> (Burgher and Shaughnessy 1986: 31)

Taking a critical perspective, it is evident that there is little, if any, sense in this description of geometric thinking being relevant outside mathematics. The higher levels appear to be (at level 3) exemplified by Euclidean geometry and then (at level 4) a consideration of non-Euclidean geometries. Yet, almost every aspect of modern life is infused with the outcomes of geometric thinking. In cities, particularly, we live in a world that has been geometrically designed; from our clothes, to our food (e.g., no wonky carrots allowed on supermarket shelves), to our cars, our roads, our furniture, our buildings, our phones. Every design choice requires reasoning about shape, but not necessarily within the kind of logical framework envisaged by van Hiele. In designing anything, there are geometrical decisions to be made about: type, quality and quantity of materials used (and hence the energy required in production); ease of packing or transport (both of the materials and the finished product); aesthetics; ease of recycling, to name but a few decisions that have implications for the planet.

A critical perspective on geometry (taken to be reasoning about shape and space) might use the tools of geometrical thinking to raise awareness of how we are manipulated by consumerism. Designs are marketed and, increasingly so, to children. There is an academic literature on children as consumers (see, for example, Gunter and Furnham 1998). In general, it is easier to see how groups of people to which we do not belong are manipulated by advertising and design. It is harder, perhaps, to spot how we are influenced in our own behaviours and choices. By looking at effects on others we may become sensitised to notice the same in ourselves.

Some of the tasks in this chapter are offered in the context of such a wider exploration of issues such as the influence of marketing. Possibilities for geometric thinking, in terms of the van Hiele levels, are highlighted in places. Linking back to Chapter 7, some of the key planning questions that have informed these lesson ideas have been around the potential in teaching geometry for collaborative learning and encouraging learners to express and examine their own views, become involved in their own learning and pose their own problems.

The activities that follow also offer the possibility of extensions into the calculus. The techniques of the calculus are met usually in the later years of schooling as a set of procedures, but there is substantial evidence that much younger students 'can get an early start thinking about these ideas, and not have to memorise a lot of formulas and notations without much understanding' (Cohen 1988: iii). Non-linear problems, such as the ones below, can lead to the contemplation of relationships through use of a spreadsheet or graphing. Often there is a maximum or minimum point that represents an optimal solution, this is the point where the graph turns. A motivating question is then, 'Can we could find a general way of calculating the place(s) on the graph where the gradient is zero?'. Differentiation provides such a general technique, by giving an expression for the gradient of a curve; equating this to zero and solving generates the turning points.

Activity 1: Energy-saving design

An obvious place for students to begin thinking critically about the geometry and sustainability of designs that are around them is through a focus on school buildings and their energy efficiency, (in the UK, this could be linked to the 'My Green School' initiative, see Open City n.d.).

Part of taking seriously the effect of human action on the planet is to consider the ways in which buildings can be made more energy efficient. In cold climates, heat is lost from the building through the walls. In hot climates, heat is transferred into the building through the walls. In both cases, the need is to minimise the surface area of the building while still enclosing the desired volume. In other words, there is a need to minimise the ratio of surface area to volume.

Students can be given the task of assessing the efficiency of the design of buildings around them (in the UK, since 2003, there has been a government-funded 'sustainable schools' initiative, see Sustainability and Environmental Education, n.d.). What is the surface area to volume ratio of students' school buildings? This will involve measurement of lengths and heights and probably a sketch of the building(s). How efficient is the building? They may, for instance, be able to access data on the school's energy efficiency. Students could compare their own school buildings to other schools locally (and their energy efficiency) or else to schools they can find out about on the web.

In order to assess the efficiency of the particular design in their school, students can turn to working on the problem of minimising surface area to volume in a more theoretical manner.

Starting point

Given a desired volume of 48m³, find some different designs of building (ignore windows and doors for now) that could achieve that volume. Find the surface area of your buildings (including the floor area). Can you find the minimum surface area?

Typical first responses from students to this challenge might be to consider a set of cuboids with volume 48m³ and find the surface area, see Figure 11.1.

Students can be supported, where necessary, in finding possibilities by being provided with cubes or isometric paper. One interesting question is the number of possible cuboids of volume 48m³, with integer sides.

A table of results can be used to share and record solutions from the class. If students record their answers on a common board at the front (e.g., with their initials next to their answer for surface area) then differences in results may emerge, which can be worked on; some possible responses are in Table 11.1.

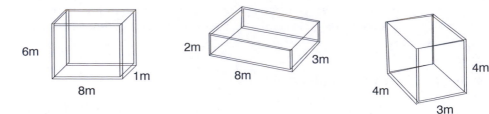

Figure 11.1   Three possible cuboids with volume 48m³

Table 11.1 Some cuboids with volume 48m³

Length (m)	Width (m)	Height (m)	Volume (m³)	Surface area (m²)	Surface area to volume ratio
8	6	1	48	114	2.4
8	3	2	48	92	1.9
3	4	4	48	80	1.7

Students may notice that the more like a cube the shape, the lower the surface area to volume ratio, leading to a decimal search for the cube root of 48.

$4 \times 4 \times 4 = 64$ too big

$3 \times 3 \times 3 = 27$ too small

$3.5 \times 3.5 \times 3.5 = \cdots$

For a rectangular design, the cube is the most efficient building in terms of minimising surface area to volume. In practice, considerations of the need for light and ventilation mean this shape is rarely used due to the energy saving that comes from natural light and ventilation over the course of the lifetime of a building. A striking exception to this rule is the black 'cube' built for the University of Sheffield (UK), as a music practice and studio space where rooms require insulation from outside noise; photographs of this building can be found by searching for images on the web (e.g., Dezeen 2008).

Possibilities

Having noticed that a regular shape offers the minimal surface area among cuboids, students may want to look at other possible regular shapes as solutions; for example, a tetrahedron, half of an octahedron or a hemisphere (for the latter two, the full shape would not be stable) (Figure 11.2).

For the shapes in Figure 11.2, the challenge becomes finding side lengths that will create a volume of 48m³ in the first place. Students may need to be given some formulae below in order to be able to choose a side length or radius and then calculate the volume. They may be able to work out some of these formulae for themselves:

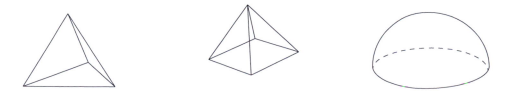

Figure 11.2 A tetrahedron, a half octahedron (square-based pyramid) and hemisphere

- volume of a pyramid $= \dfrac{1}{3} \times$ base area $\times$ height

- area of an equilateral triangle $= \sqrt{\dfrac{3}{2}} \times$ length^2 (which can be found using Pythagoras)

- vertical height of a tetrahedron $= \dfrac{\sqrt{2}}{\sqrt{3}} \times$ length (slightly trickier to work out!)

- vertical height of a half octahedron $= \dfrac{1}{\sqrt{2}} \times$ length (requires Pythagoras to derive)

- volume of a sphere $= \dfrac{4}{3}\pi r^3$

- surface area of a sphere $= 4\pi r^2$

The students could use a decimal search to get side lengths that give a volume close to 48m³, or perhaps derive and re-arrange a formula and solve it. Students may discover that the hemisphere is the most efficient design, discovered by Eskimos in an environment where conserving heat is essential for survival (Figure 11.3).

At this point, it may be that students can return to their original findings about their own school and get more of a sense of the efficiency of their buildings compared to some optimal solutions they have considered from a surface area and volume perspective. Perhaps a new extension or building is being planned? Students could summarise their findings and write to those concerned. It may be that they cannot affect the shape of their buildings but they could look into what else could be done to reduce energy consumption. For example, there are often old and inefficient heating systems in schools. It would be possible to research the cost of installing a new system and projected savings in fuel bills, in order to find the number of years to repay the investment. It may be possible to interview the person responsible for the school or district budget and ask questions about what prevents this kind of investment. There are opportunities for modes of thinking that get close to van Hiele's level 4 (deduction) if students are able to make arguments based on current data and projections into the future. There is scope for work on literacy if students send a letter to a local politician with a summary of their findings and questions or recommendations for action.

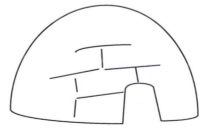

Figure 11.3 A hemispherical igloo

Where this can go

Leading on from considerations of eco-design of building shape, students might also be interested in other features of buildings that can make a significant difference to their energy efficiency. One good example of such a feature is the extent to which buildings make best use of the sun's heat (passive solar design). The issues vary depending on the climactic conditions; for example, in cooler climates it is important to provide shade in summer (to avoid the need for energy-hungry air conditioning) and as much light as possible in the winter (to minimise lighting and heating needs).

To support this work, as a teacher you will need to either research yourself, or set as a task for students, finding the maximum and minimum angles made by the sun and the ground for your location, i.e., the angles at mid-summer and mid-winter (see Further Reading at the end of this chapter for a website that provides this information).

At its simplest, students could consider the optimal roof overhang of a south-facing wall with a roof pitch of 45 degrees. In Figure 11.4, the maximum sun angle is 69 degrees and the minimum 13 degrees. The task for students is to design the overhang and window size so that, at its height, no summer sun enters the building and, at its lowest, the maximum winter sun does. The task for the teacher is to decide how many measurements to give students and how many to leave as choices in a diagram such as Figure 11.4. For younger students, the problem could be approached by scale-drawing. For older students, the approach might be using trigonometry. One simplification would be to model the roof and walls as lines.

Student solutions can, again, be compared to different local buildings and/or recommendations made regarding any new buildings in the school.

Another possibility, if students get into the idea of energy saving, is to try and persuade the relevant authorities to have an 'energy free' day in school. There would be no computers, no lights, no heating, no cooked food – students could see how much energy and money is saved. A school could obviously not run, in the long term, on no energy so such a day is not about an image of a sustainable future but more about raising awareness of the use of resources. You might want to keep data on energy use before and after the day to see if there has been any impact on behaviour in the short or long term.

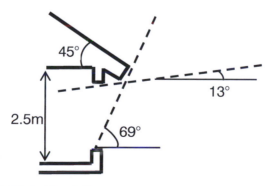

Figure 11.4 Passive solar design

Activity 2: The drinks business

Canned drinks are big business. An estimated 475 billion drink cans are produced globally each year. A reformation approach (see Chapter 1) to teaching mathematics might take the quantity of cans produced as the context for the problem of minimising the quantity of metal used, in order to provoke work on cylinders, areas and volumes (as described in more detail below). A transformation approach might instead begin with a focus on any of the big drinks manufacturers and their influence. For example, before the first lesson on this topic, students could be given an assignment to research criticisms, both positive and negative, about one of the big drinks companies. The lesson could begin with a sharing of information and sources. Issues likely to arise include: size of company; profits; donations to 'good causes'; health effects (for example, decisions about sugar levels); marketing (for example, to children); labour practices; pesticides in products; environmental record; proportion recycled. Taking a critical stance to the source of the information collected will be crucial since there are many vested interests affecting the reliability of information. Research may be needed to corroborate sources. A discussion of what students have found out could lead to an agreement about some questions for collective investigation.

Starting point

Another, perhaps less controversial, direction for this project is a consideration of the efficiency of the design of cans in terms of the amount of metal needed. Invite students to bring in a can or bottled drink. Students could begin by measuring the cans they have brought in, calculating the surface area to volume ratio. The lower the ratio, the more efficient the design.

Possibilities

This task can be varied considerably. At the open end of the spectrum, students can be invited to come up with their own design of container, combining some or all of the needs for: minimising material use; making it handleable; aesthetics; efficiency of packing. A more constrained version would limit students to only considering cylinders. Students could be given a fixed volume (500cm³, say) and invited to find the cylinder that minimises surface area.

Students may need support in being able to find a cylinder with a given volume. A cylinder has two variables, its radius and its height. One of these needs to be fixed, the other can then be calculated to ensure the volume is, say, 500cm³.

The volume of a cylinder $= \pi r^2 h$

So, if you fix r and want a volume of 500cm³, you get $h = 500 / (\pi r^2)$

If you fix h and want a volume of 500cm³, you get $r = \sqrt{(500 / \pi h)}$

If a student went down the route of choosing different values of r, something like Table 11.2 might emerge.

The optimal solution can be compared to commercial cans and bottles. Students could try to find examples of commercial products that are far from this optimum. Why

Table 11.2 Finding the optimal cylinder

Radius (cm)	Area of base (πr^2)	Height 500/(πr^2)	Volume (cm³)	Surface area (cm²)	Surface area to volume ratio
1	3.14	159.24	500	506.3	1.01
2	12.56	39.81	500	275.1	0.55
3	28.26	17.69	500	223.2	0.45

might a company choose to make, for example, a taller, thinner can than the optimum? Presumably the reason is considerations of creating a unique 'look' and brand recognition of the product? Is this worth the cost in terms of the environment? A letter could be written to the company setting out the case for a more efficient design. In moving beyond the mathematics curriculum, students could research where the materials for soft drink cans come from and some of the political issues around their production; for example, what proportion of profits go to the producers of the raw materials?

Where this can go

What area (stacked one high) or volume would 475 billion cans take up? Can this be compared to anything known?

There are possibilities for further information gathering and comparison of sugar or fructose content or caffeine levels of different drinks. There may be drink dispensers in the school or a local sports centre and students could request information about these machines. How much is the school/centre paid? What control is there over the drinks sold? How long is the contract? When were soft drinks first sold here? What other possibilities are there for drinks dispensing? Which ones were considered? Why was this one chosen? Representations can be made to school or other authorities about the range of drinks available. At a more immediate level, a survey could be done of the proportion of cans recycled by the school to those put in general waste. Are some bins not used well? Is there an issue in terms of where they are placed? Or how many there are? Students could do a survey of where litter is dropped at the end of one break-time. There would be scope for abstract geometrical thinking if students, for example, engaged in reasoning about better bin positioning.

Activity 3: Efficient packing

This task could be an extension to Activity 2, if students were to consider the efficiency with which containers could be packaged for transport. There are obvious environmental implications here in terms of reducing the size of the carbon footprint required to put products on shop shelves.

Starting point

Imagine a lorry full of packaged products. It is in everyone's interest that the products stack efficiently, so that there is as little wasted space as possible, minimising the number of journeys needed to transport goods from one place to another and reducing the carbon footprint of transportation.

We can begin by just looking at the cross-section, or the floor plan of the packaging.

What suggestions does anyone have for shapes that can pack leaving no space? (The mathematical word for this kind of arrangement is a tessellation.)

Students are likely to come up with the idea of square or rectangular packaging. Some may also be aware of the hexagonal pattern of honeycomb. There are various choices for where this task could be taken.

Possibilities

If students come up with the idea of a quadrilateral package, the question could be posed, are there other quadrilaterals that can tessellate? If students explore this, the question may turn into: is there a quadrilateral shape that does *not* tessellate? A similar problem could be posed for triangular shapes. Students could explore these challenges and try to draw out sections of tessellations for shapes they choose. Shapes that they think may not work can be collected on a common board that will become challenges for the rest of the class. It is important that students do not worry about the edges of any fixed space that they are trying to pack. Part of this challenge can be to think about the minimum information needed to specify a particular tessellation. For example, the shapes in Figure 11.5 might be seen to specify a tessellation in two directions, that can therefore cover the plane. Could this be specified with fewer shapes?

If students choose to explore triangular packaging footprints, one challenge can be to try and construct (using a pair of compasses) the different tessellations they find.

Where this can go

Another route for investigation can be tessellations involving regular shapes. If just one regular shape is allowed, it may surprise students that the only possibilities are triangles, squares and hexagons. Proofs of this are accessible, for example considering the interior

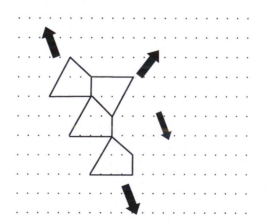

Figure 11.5 Specifying a tessellation

angles of the regular polygons (together with the insight that you would need at least three of any shape to meet at a point in order to make a tessellation). This becomes a purely geometric problem and could be tackled at level 2 or 3 of the van Hiele system.

A richer source of problems comes from considering the situation where you are allowed different regular polygons meeting at a point. There might be two or three different kinds of packaging that could be transported together, with no gaps.

Students can again work on this challenge through a consideration of interior angles, which will have to sum to 360 degrees around a point in order to create a tessellation. For example, you could have four equilateral triangles and one regular hexagon meeting at a point ($4 \times 60 + 120 = 360$). Not all numerical solutions will necessarily work geometrically. There are materials (for example, regular polygon 'Mathematical Activity Tiles' (MATs) all with the same side length, produced by the Association of Teachers of Mathematics in the UK) that students can use to test out ideas.

The issue of packaging is one that can be explored more broadly by students. The UK now has an Advisory Committee on Packaging (ACP), part of whose remit is to advise on optimising packaging and increasing recycling. Significant progress has been made in the UK in the last 15 years. The UK government's Department for Environment Food and Rural Affairs reports that of an estimated 10.8 million tonnes of packaging waste in the UK in 2010, 67 per cent was recovered. This compares to 1998, when only 27 per cent of total packaging waste was recovered (Defra 2012). There are targets to increase the proportion recovered in the UK to above 70 per cent by 2015 although the ACP in 2011 was arguing for tougher targets. Students could find out local recycling rates and compare these to national figures. If there are shortfalls, representation could be made to local politicians (these tasks link to Activity 2 in Chapter 4).

Another possible avenue for further work would be to consider how to make *boxes without glue*. Looking at packaging these days, it is perhaps surprising that many items (for instance, anything to do with fast food such as pizza boxes, cardboard filing boxes) can be flat-packed to minimise the volume needed in distributing the goods with consequent savings on fuel and then the nets of the boxes can be assembled when needed without any other fixing agents such as glue, staples or sellotape (a net is any 2D shape that can fold to make a 3D object). Students can be encouraged to make a collection of boxes without glue and investigate their nets, perhaps whilst also noting down any information on content of any food (see Chapter 4).

Taking a critical perspective on 'boxes without glue', we can ask questions such as who benefits from this design initiative? The packaging must use more cardboard than a simple net but perhaps is stronger? Does the extra cardboard cost less than a small amount of glue? What are the environmental costs of creating glue compared to cardboard? What other considerations are there?

For younger students, suppose you want a picture of a snake to wrap around a box (so that part of the snake shows on all six sides). Draw the snake on a net of cube and see if it fits together when you make it into a box. Design a net that will make a box without using any glue, where does the snake drawing fit on the net? Make a net for a box without glue with minimum paper or card.

For older students, the design of containers needs to take into account various criteria such as strength, amount of material used, appeal to customer, cost of manufacturing, sustainability. Some packages may be on the table, if students have been collecting examples. Look at these for ideas and make explicit the criteria you think were used in each case. Now design and make boxes to hold an Easter egg or six cream eggs and write a report on how the designs differ, given different criteria.

Activity 4: Minimal connector

There are a variety of contexts in which it is important to be able to minimise the length of a network, joining some fixed points in order to minimise use of resources or energy. This might be in wanting to create an oil pipeline that is as short as possible but which connects four towns, designing heating or plumbing systems in houses, creating a fibre-optic cable network, a network of tunnels, or on a micro-scale, connecting electronics components in a manner that minimises propagation times. Points on the network do not need to be connected directly to each other but you must be able to get from any point to any other point. The smaller the network is, the greater the environmental saving and the greater the efficiency of the system.

Starting point

Imagine four points (they could be houses, or towns, or data points) arranged at the corners of a square of side length 10km, what is the minimum network that can connect them?

Students can be invited to come to the board to share their initial guesses with the class (since the first ones are likely to be straightforward to work out, and as a teacher you will have an opportunity to assess whether students have interpreted the task in the way you want).

Initial guesses from students are often among those in Figure 11.6 (the last two provoking a need for Pythagoras' theorem).

After having a few solutions on the board, students can be invited to try and find smaller networks on their own or in groups.

Look out for anyone who begins to draw the kind of shape in Figure 11.7. You might want to work, publicly, on one of these solutions. Students may be surprised to find they are smaller than the cross.

Possibilities

Finding the lengths in Figure 11.7 can be done via Pythagoras' theorem. Students could, for example, choose the length of the middle section and then work out the other side lengths to find the length of the network (Table 11.3).

Again, a decimal search may be used to try and hone in on what length in the middle gives the minimum network overall.

An alternative approach is to choose the angle that the 'arms' make with a side of the square. This leads to a trigonometric approach that has a rather elegant solution, left as an exercise for the reader!

Figure 11.6 Typical initial solutions to the 'four towns' problem

Figure 11.7 Towards an optimal solution

Table 11.3 Finding the minimum network

Length of middle section (km)	Length of four 'arms' (km)	Overall network length (km)
1	6.73	6.73 × 4 + 1 = 26.9
2	4.47	4.47 × 4 + 2 = 19.9
3	4.61	
4		

Where this can go

This problem is one example of the general question of how to find the minimum connector between *n* points in the plane. This is called the Steiner network problem, named after the Swiss mathematician Jakob Steiner (1796–1863), even though it was first posed, for *n*=3, by Fermat in the seventeenth century (Ivanov and Tuzhilin 1994). The problem is distinct from the minimal spanning tree problem in discrete or decision mathematics, since in the Steiner network problem it is allowable to create new nodes in the solution. In general (if students use a trigonometric approach to the four towns problem they will see this), lines make 120-degree angles with each other if they are part of an optimal solution. Students could work on Fermat's version of the problem by drawing any triangle (i.e., three points in the plane) and trying to construct the minimum connector (Figure 11.8). Students could explore trying to construct a point within the triangle so that lines from the vertices to this point make three 120-degree angles (N.B. problems occur if the triangle itself has an angle over 120 degrees).

If all the angles of the triangle are less than 120 degrees, elegant constructions were found in 1640 (the Torricelli point) and 1750 (the Simpson line) to create the point

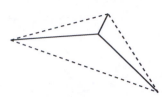

Figure 11.8 A minimum connector of 3 points, lines meeting at 120-degree angles

in question. Heinen, in 1834, extended these solutions to incorporate triangles with angles over 120 degrees. Students could research these solutions themselves having worked on the problem for a while. There are remarkable properties of Simpson lines and connections to the minimum network solution. The proofs of these connections would take students into the deductive level of geometric thinking.

Solutions to Steiner network problems can be *seen* by fixing two perspex plates, 1cm apart, and using rivets to represent the points to be connected. If the plates are dunked into a bucket of soapy water, with a little practice, a bubble will be left between the rivets as you take out the plates. In the same way a bubble in air forms the shape with minimum surface area to volume (a sphere), it does so between the rivets to form the minimal network.

Further reading

- If you are interested in exploring issues around passive solar design, there are some extraordinary tools at: http://www.sunearthtools.com. On the interactive map, students could type in their home address and see, overlaid on a satellite image, the path of the sun. There are charts and tables of information also provided, including the angle of elevation of the sun at midday.
- Many of the activities in this chapter have suggested possible projects for improving the school environment. There is a UK organisation, Eco-Schools (http://www.eco-schools.org), that supports and accredits this kind of activity.

References

Burger, W. and Shaughnessy, J. M. (1986) Characterizing the van Hiele levels of development in geometry, *Journal for Research in Mathematics Education*, 17(1): 31–48.

Cohen, D. (1988) *Calculus by and for young people (ages 7, yes 7 and up)*, Champaign, IL: Don Cohen–The Mathman.

Defra (2012) Wastes and recycling. Available at http://www.defra.gov.uk/environment/waste/ (accessed 7 Aug 2012).

Dezeen (2008) Soundhouse by Careyjones and Jefferson Sheard. Available at http://www.dezeen.com/2008/09/24/soundhouse-by-careyjones-and-jefferson-sheard/ (accessed 12 October 2012).

Ivanov, A. and Tuzhilin, A. (1994) *Minimal networks: The Steiner problem and its generalizations*. London: CRC Press.

Gunter, B. and Furnham, A. (1998) *Children as consumers: a psychological analysis of the young people's market*. London and New York: Routledge.

Open City (n.d.) My green school. Available at http://open-city.org.uk/education/schools/MyGreenSchool.html (accessed 12 October 2012).

Sustainability and Environmental Education (n.d.) Sustainable schools. Available at http://se-ed.co.uk/edu/sustainable-schools/ (accessed 12 October 2012).

van Hiele, P. (1986) *Structure and insight*. Orlando, FL: Academic Press.

Starting from probability

Richard Barwell

Probability can seem a rather marginal topic in school mathematics, a once-a-year opportunity to roll dice or flip coins multiple times. In terms of the mathematical formatting of society and our lives, however, probability turns out to be important. Probability is, for example, fundamental to the actuarial sciences, as applied in the insurance industry. Most people have insurance for such things as their house, car, possessions, health and life. The premiums we pay are calculated based on the probabilities of bad things happening. Where do these probabilities come from? Who calculates them? Who decides if they are reasonable?

Probability underpins modern medicine, risk assessment, pensions and, of course, gambling. Much of the science we accept as true is demonstrated through tests of statistical significance, tests that are based entirely on the concepts of randomness and distribution. To take just one example, the pharmaceutical industry demonstrates that a new drug has the effects that they claim by showing that more people get better when they take it than when they do not and that *this difference is very unlikely to have occurred by chance*. Unfortunately, many of the basic concepts of probability, such as the concepts of fairness, randomness and risk, are not well understood, even by adults (for example, Pratt *et al*. 2011). A critical understanding of both society and of mathematics requires greater attention to and understanding of probability.

Research on the learning of probability-related concepts and aspects of statistical literacy has come to a couple of conclusions. First, students are able to make more meaningful sense of complex data when it is about situations with which they are reasonably familiar (for example, Langrall *et al*. 2011). Armed with such familiarity, students are better able to identify which information is relevant or useful, and to understand the limits of the data and interpret it reasonably. Second, in evaluating risk, students tend, again, to draw on their own experience of situations, as much or more than making use of mathematical arguments. Pratt *et al.* (2011), for example, developed a simulation of a situation relating to medical risks associated with surgical interventions. Participants (in this case mathematics and science teachers) drew as much on their affective response (i.e., how they felt about different options) to different scenarios as they did on the mathematical and scientific information provided in the scenario. These kinds of findings suggest that students need to explore situations with which they have some connection, interest and familiarity.

The three activities included in this chapter suggest different ways in which students can engage with topics related to sustainability, using publicly available data. They look at differences in life expectancy in different countries, and at the effects of climate change. The mathematical concepts covered include the expression of probability in different forms, and the interpretation of these probabilities; frequency-based calculations of probability; and the notion of risk. Of course, different students will be interested in different things, so these activities should be seen as examples of the kinds of things that are possible. In each case, a moderate amount of prior research is needed to locate data sources and, in some cases, render them more accessible to students. For some students, it will be enough to point them to the data sources and allow them to get to work, with some guidance to keep them focused. For other students, it may be necessary to select and organise suitable data and provide them for students in a more user-friendly form.

Activity 1: How long have I got?

How old are you? How likely do you think it is that you will live another year? Does it make any difference how old you are? Or whether you live in a relatively rich country or a relatively poor one? Are you more likely to live another year if you are 20 compared with if you are 70? Or if you live in Rio de Janeiro or in Reading? These kinds of questions are about probability. Investigating them can reveal disparities in infant mortality or life expectancy around the world. These disparities have consequences for individuals and for wider society and raise further questions of equity, social justice and sustainability.

Many people have life insurance – they pay small premiums on a regular basis and if they die, their families receive a payout to compensate for the death. Life insurance is a way of managing the risks of the loss of a breadwinner in a family, so that mortgages or other debts may be paid and new sources of income found. Insurers calculate their premiums based on *life tables*, which provide probabilities, death rates and life expectancies for different populations and in relation to different behaviours. These tables are also a valuable source of information for demographers, who study population trends, and for comparing international progress on problems like infant mortality or smoking-related diseases. The incidence and severity of some of these problems varies widely between more and less developed countries. Infant mortality, for example, is much higher in poorer countries than it is in rich countries like the UK.

The activities suggested below introduce some of the elements of life tables, making use of some basic probability concepts in context, including the expression and interpretation of probabilities as a decimal, and the relationship between probability and expected frequency. The activities lead on to a comparison of life tables for Brazil and the UK, highlighting some of the disparities between life (and death) in the two countries.

Starting points

Look at the graph shown in Figure 12.1. It shows for each age up to 100 the probability of males and females in the UK dying within a year. This probability is known as $q(x)$ where x is age in years. The graph provides a good starting point for students' thinking, prompted by some questions:

■ What can you tell me about the graph?
■ Can you explain the shape of the curve?
■ When is the probability highest? Why might that be?
■ When is the probability lowest? Why might that be?
■ Why do the y-axis values not go up to 1?
■ What differences are there between males and females? How can these differences be interpreted?
■ What would a graph of the probabilities of surviving for another year look like?

Discussing the graph should lead to some discussion of the meaning of probabilities in decimal form, some interpretation of different probability values, and some awareness of the relative nature of the probabilities shown. In some cases, groups of students might work on creating a graph of the probabilities of surviving for another year.

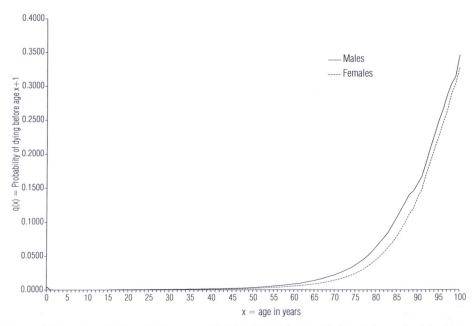

Figure 12.1 Probability of UK males and females of age x dying before reaching age x+1 (based on 2008–2010 data). Data source: Office for National Statistics, http://www.ons.gov.uk/ons/rel/lifetables/interim-life-tables/2008-2010/rft-ilt-uk-2008-2010.xls, published 29 September 2011, accessed 3 March 2013.

Possibilities

There is a relationship between $q(x)$ and the probability of surviving for the next year, known as $p(x)$. This relationship can be expressed in the following equation, which students could discuss:

$$p(x) = 1 - q(x)$$

These probabilities can then be used to calculate the chance of surviving from *birth* to a given age, known as $l(x)$. This probability is usually expressed as a number of individuals surviving out of a given starting population, typically 100,000. The relation is given by the following equation (students could be asked to generate their own equations, or to discuss this one):

$$l(x + 1) = l(x) \cdot p(x) \text{ where } l(0) = 100,000$$

Students could be asked to predict what the graph of l might look like for the data shown above. They could then be provided with the relevant data, on paper or in electronic format in order to produce the curve for themselves, or could simply be shown the graph. The curve for the above UK data is shown in Figure 12.2.

Finally, one more graph is provided: the graph of $q(x)$ for Brazil, shown in Figure 12.3.

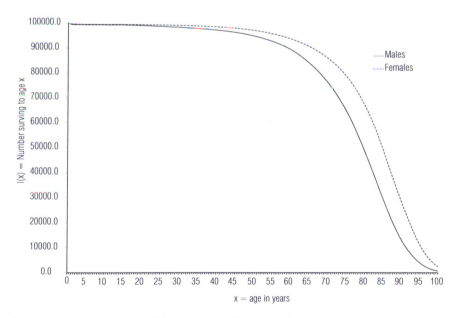

Figure 12.2 Probability of UK males and females of age x surviving to age x, expressed per 100,000 (based on 2008–2010 data). Data source: Office for National Statistics, http://www.ons.gov.uk/ons/rel/lifetables/interim-life-tables/2008-2010/rft-ilt-uk-2008-2010.xls, published 29 September 2011, accessed 3 March 2013.

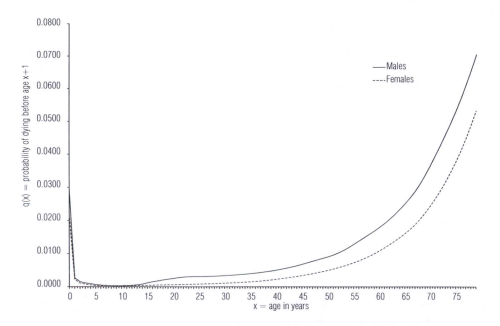

Figure 12.3 Probability of Brazil males and females of age x dying before reaching age x+1 (based on 2005 data). Data source: IBGE, Diretoria de Pesquisas (DPE), Coordenação de População e Indicadores Sociais (COPIS), downloaded from http://www.lifetable.de/data/MPIDR/BRA000020052005CU1.pdf. Accessed 2 March 2013.

At this point, discussion can be prompted by questions like:

- What is the same and what is different about the graphs for Brazil and the UK? Students will notice the different curve, but also might comment on the different ranges and probabilities and the divergence between male and female curves in early adulthood.
- What might explain these differences?
- When might it be better to be Brazilian? When might it be better to be British?

In discussing these questions, various issues could arise, including the high infant mortality rate in Brazil, male violence in some parts of society, the effects of living in a less wealthy country and class differences. Discussion of these issues should be conducted in the language of probability, frequency and statistics. Students might conclude this discussion by generating some questions to work on. They might also be prompted to discuss some of the underlying values on which the life tables approach depends. For example, how do students feel about a quantitative approach that aggregates data across populations? The statistic that you have a low chance of dying in your twenties is little comfort to the families of the few people who die in road traffic accidents or of rare diseases. And, for another example, should the information that young people in the UK are very unlikely to die affect students' behaviour? Does it mean that they can engage in risky behaviour without fear of negative consequences? This last issue is linked to an important point about probability: it describes a general likelihood, not a specific event.

Where might this go?

Having established some starting points, such as the use of life-table data and of comparison, students could investigate data from other countries, although their questions may be even broader, taking in, for example, income data. Life-table data is readily available online, although some work is needed to present it in an accessible form. For the above activities, only $q(x)$ data were extracted from larger tables and entered into a spreadsheet. The website 'Human Life-Table Database' (http://www.lifetable.de) is a portal linking to government life tables from around the world. These data are not always easily compared; they relate to different time periods, for example. These issues could be discussed by students.

Often, multiple tables are provided for a country for different periods. One interesting investigation might look at changes over time for a single country. The website 'Understanding Uncertainty' (http://understandinguncertainty.org) has animated graphs of $l(x)$ for a range of countries making visual comparisons relatively straightforward. 'Understanding Uncertainty' also has animations (for the UK showing $q(x)$ that takes into account four different behaviours: smoking, diet, exercise and alcohol consumption). An exploration of these animations could lead to students thinking about their own lifestyles and considering the choices they may already have made (for example, to smoke) or may make in the future.

Activity 2: Frost and farming

Winter frost can be magical: sparkling ice crystals on a cold, clear winter morning when your breath clouds in the air in front of you. But not everyone appreciates frost, at least not all the time. Farmers and gardeners watch out for frost because of the damage it can cause to plants. Some crops benefit from frost (parsnips taste sweeter after a frost) and others are hardy enough to withstand the cold temperatures. But some crops can be damaged. Spring is a particularly crucial time. If fruit trees begin to blossom during a warm spell and are then hit by frost, much of the blossom is destroyed and much less fruit is produced. As a result, the presence or absence of frost can have economic implications. Here is what the Royal Horticultural Society said recently about frost:

> The Royal Horticultural Society (RHS) is concerned that this year's mild winter may lead to smaller fruit crops this autumn with a subsequent rise in prices.
>
> Most hardy fruit plants need a period of chilling during winter in order to encourage flowering. Without this cold effect evidence from previous years shows that crops may be reduced. Blackcurrants, cherries and some apple cultivars have a particularly high chilling requirement.
>
> The other potential problem is that if there is not a prolonged cold period plants will start growing earlier than normal and may flower early too. This could put them at a greater risk of damage if there is frost during April and early May. Early flowering may also mean less fruit being set as there may be fewer pollinating insects around. The current cold spell may help but RHS fruit experts suggest

that a colder and longer spell of weeks would better ensure that any growth and flowering development is held back.

(RHS press release, 18 January 2012)

So how likely is frost in, say, the critical month of April? Is climate change having any impact on frost in April? The activities below suggest some ways that an aspect of weather like frost could be investigated. These activities particularly involve frequency-based models of probability.

Starting points

Read the RHS press release, shown above. What questions arise? How could they be investigated? Let's keep the focus on frost. How could the likelihood of frost be investigated? Unlike probability about dice or games, it would be more or less impossible to work out a theoretical probability of frost. The approach must, therefore, be based on frequency data. Students could discuss what kind of data they would need and how they would use that data. Alternatively, students could be provided with a data set and asked to discuss how they could use the data it contains. For example, Table 12.1 shows *part* of a data set for Leuchars, in Scotland, from the Met Office website. Only the recorded data for days of air frost ('af days') are shown. An air frost is recorded when the air temperature falls below 0°C at, typically, 1.2m above ground level. The full data set for Leuchars runs from 1957 right up to 2012 and includes several other measures.

Given this kind of data, how could questions about frost be investigated? Students could generate questions, such as:

- How likely is frost?
- In which months is frost most or least likely?
- How likely is frost in summer? How likely is a frost-free winter?
- How likely are extreme cold events (e.g. temperatures below –10°C)?
- How does the likelihood of frost vary in different parts of the country?
- Have probabilities of frost or cold weather changed in recent decades?

To calculate probabilities using frequency data like that shown in Table 12.1, the following ratio is used:

p(event) = frequency of occurrence of event / number of possible occurrences

At this point, then, some decisions need to be made about what 'event' to focus on and about what time period should be used to calculate the probability of the event. Students could generate and consider different alternatives and discuss what difference these choices might make. If the decisions is to focus on the likelihood of an 'af' day in Leuchars in April, it would be important to discuss over how long a period the frequencies of frost in April (for example) should be examined. Would a calculation based on the data for 1957 be reasonable?

Table 12.1 Frost days in Leuchars, Scotland, 1957–1958

Year	Month	Air frost days	Year	Month	Air frost days
1957	1	7	1958	1	16
1957	2	15	1958	2	14
1957	3	0	1958	3	15
1957	4	1	1958	4	4
1957	5	0	1958	5	0
1957	6	0	1958	6	0
1957	7	0	1958	7	0
1957	8	0	1958	8	0
1957	9	0	1958	9	0
1957	10	0	1958	10	0
1957	11	4	1958	11	4
1957	12	9	1958	12	8

$p(\text{frost in April}) = \text{number of frost days in April 1957/number of days in April}$

$$= 1 / 30$$

$$= 0.03$$

Is this reasonable? What would happen if the data for 1958 are used instead?

$p(\text{frost in April}) = \text{number of frost days in April 1958/number of days in April}$

$$= 4 / 30$$

$$= 0.13$$

The choice of year affects the probability estimate by a factor of four. How can this be addressed? The standard method is to use longer time periods. For example, all the data from 1957–2011 could be used. Students could experiment by calculating probabilities of frost in, say, the month of April, using different reference periods (e.g. 10 years, 20 years, 30 years). Comparing results and discussing differences between them across the class would lead to a reasonable class estimate of the probability of frost in April.

Possibilities

Using a period of around 10 years would allow for a reasonable estimate of probability and would also allow for an examination of variation over time. For example, using the Leuchars data, probabilities for frost in April could be computed using a spreadsheet for successive overlapping (running) 10-year periods. The outcome of such a calculation is shown in Figure 12.4.

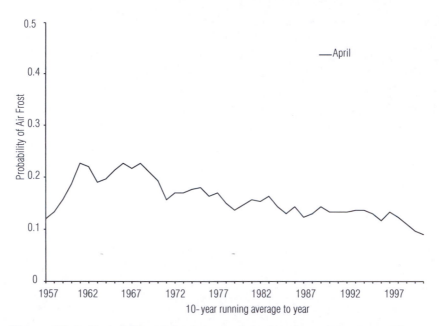

Figure 12.4 Probability of frost in April in Leuchars based on 10-year moving averages 1957–2010 (data source: http://www.metoffice.gov.uk/climate/uk/stationdata/leucharsdata.txt)

These calculations show a declining probability of frost in April in Leuchars: it seems to roughly halve from 0.2 (i.e. one in five for any given day) to 0.1 (one in ten) over the past 50 years. This decline seems to be another indication of the effect of climate change in the UK. The trend could be formalised by applying a line of best fit or other similar strategy and could lead to discussion of possible future trends. Students could discuss what this finding means in terms of the likelihood of frost, as well as the possible reasons for the changes and actions they could take to find out more.

In a similar way, probabilities could be calculated for other months, other locations and other weather phenomena so that comparisons can be made. Is the decline in the probability of frost only apparent for April, or are there changes for other months? (It turns out that there is a decline for most of the months in which frost occurs, although the strength of the decline varies.) Is the decline apparent at other locations? Are there similar declines in the probability of extreme cold? What difference does the latitude of the location make?

An important mathematical idea that arises with this kind of work is the difference between a probability and a prediction. We cannot say how much frost there will be next April, nor on which days; we can only estimate the probability of frost. From year to year, some Aprils will have many days of frost, others very few. Similarly, productive discussions could focus on how the nature of weather would affect short-term probabilities. If there is a frost on 1 April, for example, is the probability of frost on the 2 April less, the same, or higher, than the probability for the month as a whole? Frost

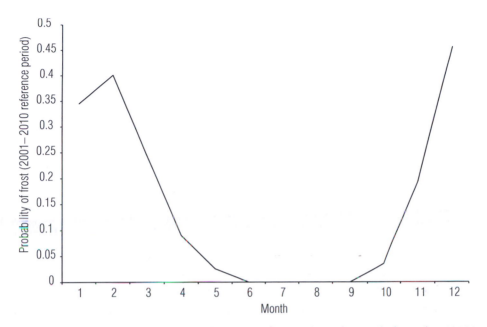

Figure 12.5 Probability of frost in Leuchars, Scotland, each month, based on 2001–2010 data

on one day may indicate a zone of cooler air, which could indicate a few days of frost. Finally, students might consider how the probability of frost might change through the month. Intuitively, the probability of frost in April declines somewhat from the beginning to the end of the month, but the calculations above give a probability for the whole month. One strategy to investigate this would be to plot the probabilities for all the months as shown in Figure 12.5.

Where might this go?

This topic presents opportunities for cross-curricular work in science and geography. Use of more detailed, and preferably local, data sets could lead to more nuanced calculations. Students could then investigate potential impact on local farming or horticulture, including in their own gardens, if they have them. This work could include contacting farmers or farming organisations to get information about crops, costs and so on. As a result of their work, students could prepare reports about frost (or other weather) to share with these organisations. Or they could prepare reports about the impact of frost on farming and horticulture to share with other students, family and the wider community. More ambitiously and transformationally (in Renert's, 2011, terms – see Chapter 1), students could communicate with decision makers to express any concerns they have about issues like climate change, citing the impact on the local economy that climate change may have. For example, students could compile reports of their analyses and send them to local councillors or MPs and invite them to visit their school to discuss their findings. They could also publish their findings on the internet and contact local experts (for example, someone from the RHS or a climate scientist at a local university) and invite them to visit their school as well. In this way, students' mathematical work can feed into local and national debates about how our society responds to climate change.

Activity 3: Should I wear wellington boots?

Every year, somewhere in the UK, flooding happens. It can be caused by unusually high tides, heavy rain leading to rivers bursting their banks, or excess surface water run-off. For instance, in recent years, floods have made the news in Aberystwyth in Wales, Cockermouth in Cumbria and Bournemouth in Dorset. Flooding can be extremely damaging, both for individuals and businesses. Flooding can render homes uninhabitable, destroy crops, disrupt roads and power-lines, and threaten power stations and other important installations. Of course some flooding has less impact: flooding of salt-water marshes or river meadows can even be beneficial in some ways. So how can decisions be made about what to try to protect – where to construct flood defences, for example – and what to leave? These kinds of decisions involve the concept of risk. The activity outlined below explores the nature of risk and its relationship to probability and allows students to consider how environmental change, along with their socio-economic status, may affect their perception of risk.

Starting points

The context for this activity is flooding. One way to begin would be to show students one or two news reports of recent flood events, particularly if they are in the region in which students live. Students could also discuss some initial questions about two or three local places with varying likelihood and potential impacts of flooding (e.g., one on high ground, one by a river or coastline, one more populated than the other etc.):

- How likely is a flood in location A, B or C?
- How bad could such a flood be in each location?
- If you had enough money from the government to build flood protections in *one* of the locations, which would you choose and why?

If the locations are well chosen, students would need to debate issues like whether it is better to protect, for example, a populated area at relatively low probability of flooding or a less populated area with a high probability of flooding. In dealing with these issues, they are talking about *risk*.

There are many ways of defining risk. This activity focuses on a mathematical approach, as commonly used by government and planning agencies. A statistical definition of risk is as follows:

Risk $= p$(accident) $\times$ (expected loss if the accident occurs)

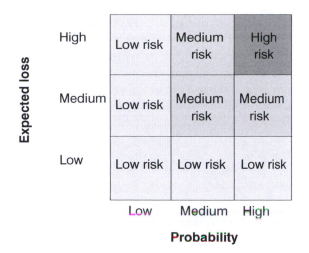

Figure 12.6 Graphic representation of risk as probability × expected loss

Expected loss could be measured in financial terms, but could be measured in other ways, for example lives lost, or could simply be estimated on a qualitative scale (low, medium, high). Probability of accidents like flooding can be estimated based on previous occurrences or calculated using mathematical models. In the case of flooding, such estimates are calculated by the Environment Agency and can be accessed at their website (Environment Agency 2013a). The graphic shown in Figure 12.6 is a simple way to think about the above definition of risk. Students could examine the graphic and discuss what it means. They could come up with examples for the different cells and could be asked to apply it to their discussion of the flooding scenarios at locations A, B and C.

Possibilities

The Environment Agency website includes estimates of the probability of flooding for the whole of the UK, through their 'Flood Map' feature. By zooming in to specific locations and clicking on the map, users can obtain an estimate of the likelihood of flooding for the selected location. The likelihood is expressed as low, moderate or significant, with sites at no risk returning no estimate. The probabilities associated with these likelihoods are as follows (Environment Agency 2013b):

- Low: less than 0.005 (1 in 200)
- Moderate: between 0.005 and 0.013 (1 in 200 to 1 in 75)
- Significant: greater than 0.013 (1 in 75)

Students could discuss the meaning of these probabilities. Why, for example, is 1 in 75 years considered significantly likely? It does not sound very high.

Students could then check the probabilities for several locations, perhaps specified in advance. To calculate risk, as opposed to likelihood, data on 'expected loss' is also needed. One possible source of data is the land registry website, which provides information on property prices. For example, for a city like Bristol, it provides the average property prices for four types of property (detached, semi, terraced, maisonette/ flat), as well as for all types taken together. By combining this kind of information with the flood likelihoods, students could generate estimates of risk. Some groups may be able to work at this kind of task with a fair degree of autonomy; others may need more support, including, for example, being provided with data for a range of locations.

Having evaluated flood risks for a range of locations, students could address some of the underlying values associated with their calculations. For example, is the choice of property values the best way to evaluate expected loss? This choice would show more affluent areas as being more at risk than less affluent areas. The latter may, however, be more densely populated. Perhaps population density could be used as an index of expected loss instead. More fundamentally, the use of a mathematical formula for risk can be interrogated. Does it make sense to simply multiply probability of flooding by expected loss? What does this kind of approach help to do and what does it overlook? A formula is easier to calculate, for example, allowing rapid assessments across large data sets, but risk is also about people's lives. The value of someone's home is not simply financial, it is emotional and personal.

Where might this go?

As with the previous activities in this chapter, there is considerable scope for cross-curricular work, with a link to geography being the most obvious. Students could develop extended work on flood defences and explore the topic of flooding as another aspect of climate change. For example, students could use historical weather data from the same sources mentioned in the 'frost and farming' activity to estimate the probability of extreme rainfall events in specific locations. They could work to decide a definition of 'extreme' and then calculate probabilities based on long-term historical data. In the same way as the probability of frost was calculated, trends in these probabilities over time could be examined. Extreme rainfall events are becoming more common. Students should be able to see this from the data. Such findings, coupled with information about population changes, would lead to some consideration of how flood risks might change in the light of climate change. Again, students could report this information in their community or communicate with decision makers to express any concerns that may arise.

Further reading

- Human Life-Table database website is a portal linking to life-table data for a wide range of countries: http://www.lifetable.de/
- Understandinguncertaity.org is about risk and uncertainty and is run by David Spiegelhalter, Winton Professor for the Public Understanding of Risk at the University of Cambridge. It includes various fascinating animations and activities that illustrate risk-related ideas, including life-table animations, but also lottery simulations and several others: http://understandinguncertainty.

org/files/animations/SurvivalWorldwide1/SurvivalWorldwide.html;   http://
understandinguncertainty.org/view/animations

■   The UK Met Office website includes publicly accessible weather data archives
    for a wide range of locations in the UK. Go to http://www.metoffice.gov.uk/
    climate/uk/stationdata/

■   The UK's Environment Agency provides information about flood risks across the
    UK, including estimates of flood probabilities and flood risks. They also helpfully
    explain what these concepts mean and how they are applied: www.environment-
    agency.gov.uk/homeandleisure/floods/default.aspx;   www.environment-agency.
    gov.uk/homeandleisure/floods/56822.aspx

References

Environment Agency (2013a) Flood. Available online at www.environment-agency.gov.uk/
    homeandleisure/floods/default.aspx.

Enviroment Agency (2013b) Flood likelihood explained. Available online at http://www.
    environment-agency.gov.uk/homeandleisure/floods/56822.aspx.

Langrall, C., Nisbet, S., Mooney, E. and Jansem, S. (2011) The role of context expertise when
    comparing data, *Mathematical Thinking and Learning,* 13(1 and 2): 47–67.

Pratt, D., Ainley, J., Kent, P., Levinson, R., Yogui, C. and Kapadia, R. (2011) Role of context in
    risk-based reasoning, *Mathematical Thinking and Learning,* 13(4): 322–45.

Renert, M. (2011) Mathematics for life: sustainable mathematics education, *For the Learning of
    Mathematics,* 31(1) 20–6.

Royal Horticultural Society (2011) Press release. Available online at http://press.rhs.org.uk/
    Press-releases.aspx?view=all.

Conclusion
The planet matters – does mathematics teaching?

In the preceding chapters, we have argued that mathematics teachers can address issues of sustainability in their teaching and we have suggested some ways in which this could be achieved. We have not sought to provide a set of off-the-shelf mathematics lessons. Integrating sustainability issues into mathematics teaching requires an approach that responds to our students' interests and concerns. Negotiating and debating what will be studied and how it will be studied is risky, challenging, and the outcome may be difficult to predict, but these qualities are an important part of a democratic, transformative approach to mathematics teaching. Instead of presenting ready-made activities, then, we have explored some sustainability topics that interest and concern us. We hope that the ideas we have included show how such topics can be developed, through a little background research, perhaps with the support of a collaborative group of colleagues, into viable teaching ideas. While we would be delighted if readers are inspired by the ideas included in this book to develop them further into activities for use in their own classrooms, we would be even more delighted if readers were inspired to explore topics with their students that we have not been able to include.

In the reflective spirit of critical mathematics education, the rest of this concluding chapter is devoted to two things. First, we draw out what were, for us, a couple of important themes running through the book. Second, we reflect on our work through a discussion of some challenging questions that arose through the course of our work. These questions are about issues that are implicit in our writing but that we have, perhaps, skirted around. Can our teaching really make a difference? What are the limits of what our teaching, or students' actions, or mathematics itself can achieve? Does teaching mathematics really matter that much?

Common themes

We have developed our ideas and written this book from the perspective of critical mathematics education (Skovsmose 1984). A theme running throughout the first section is Skovsmose's notion of the formatting power of mathematics: Mathematics is not a neutral tool for modelling and controlling the world; it is part of the structure of our society. A critical mathematics education attempts to offer students some insight into how this structuring takes place and the consequences it can have. Some examples of the formatting power of mathematics from the first part of the book include:

- the role of the Black–Scholes equation in derivatives trading;
- the influence of climate models on national and international debates about climate change;
- the selection and presentation of information included in food labels;
- the social, economic and environmental consequences of flaws in the modelling of fish stocks;
- the human choices and human consequences embedded in calculations of unemployment figures.

In each case, mathematics has marked social consequences: in the formulation of policy, in the behaviour of organisations, or in the tangible impacts on individuals. Mathematics is not a physical cause of climate change, for example, but it drives the technologically powered, industrialised consumer society that *is* changing the climate of our planet.

In each of our examples, it is apparent that the role of mathematics in shaping our world is often invisible. If our students are to contribute to the development of a more sustainable future, it seems to us that they need to understand the role of mathematics, both in the society in which we currently live, and in shaping the society in which *they* will live.

In each example, it is also apparent how mathematics is, as Skovsmose (1984) observed, embedded in technology. The aura of neutrality that is often attributed to both mathematics and technology hides the important human work that goes into constructing mathematical models and the computer systems that depend on them. Worse, they can be used to further particular interests. Mathematical models of fish stocks, for example, seemed to justify continued levels of fishing that turned out to be unsustainable. This modelling aligned conveniently well with various economic and political interests, including those of the fishing industry (in the short term).

Some practical answers to how we might use mathematics to support the planet, at least in a classroom context, were offered in the second section of the book. A strong theme in these chapters is that collaborative ways of working and an emphasis on critical reflection are key elements of a critical mathematics education approach. This collaborative ethos is in evidence in many of the classroom activities we have outlined, including, for example, the Trading Game (Chapter 2), the suggestions for data-handling projects (Chapter 8), or the group task on recycling (Figure 10.1).

Our ideas also illustrate the many opportunities for cross-curricular working. Here are some possibilities:

- the 'if the world were a village' activity in Chapter 8 connects with personal, social and health education, and drama;
- the population modelling in Chapter 9 connects with biology;
- the green space activity in Chapter 10 connects with geography;
- the energy saving activity in Chapter 11 connects with physics, and design and technology;
- the 'frost and farming' activity in Chapter 12 connects with geography.

More generally, the transformational approach that can be applied to all of our ideas implies a more thorough-going integrated approach to the curriculum, with students drawing on multiple curriculum areas in the course of understanding an issue and then seeking to take action. A project on pollution in the neighbourhood of the school, for example, would clearly involve mathematics (e.g. in collecting and interpreting different kinds of data), but may also involve chemistry (e.g. of pollutants), physics (e.g. relating to weather), biology (e.g. effects on life), history (e.g. changes in economic activity in the neighbourhood), literature (e.g. fiction that examines pollution), literacy (e.g. preparing reports and communicating with decision-makers), physical education (e.g. effects of pollution on performance) and so on. Such projects are complex and challenging and depend on widespread collaboration between teachers and students. If they are to be transformative, they also require students to take responsibility and teachers to support them to do so.

Of course, a transformative approach may not always be possible. However, even within the boundaries of a traditional mathematics curriculum and classroom, collaboration, reflection and questioning can all be integrated into students' work. A feature of many of the activities in this book has been a focus on students making choices, posing their own problems and having the space to work on these problems. As well as critical mathematics education having implications for the kind of content we offer, then, there are also implications for a *way* of working.

It can seem an impossible task to stay abreast of current issues. We have been struck, during the period of writing this book, just how quickly some of the issues have moved on. However, this uncertainty can be an advantage, in terms of taking a critical perspective. It becomes even more important and obvious that we need to question sources and motives. The pace of change means that the only possibility, if we are to teach as if the planet matters, is to work collaboratively, to share our research and findings, and to critique each other.

Unanswered questions

Can our teaching really make a difference? What are the limits of what our teaching, or students' actions, or mathematics itself can achieve? Does teaching mathematics really matter that much? These questions are related to the broader debate about whether individual choices can have an impact on global sustainability issues. Do, for example, actions like buying organic food, recycling and composting waste, or choosing a fuel-efficient car have an impact on the sustainability of the planetary ecosystem? The answer, of course, is both yes and no. Buying organic food may encourage farming practices that are likely to promote greater biodiversity. On the other hand, if the food is first transported great distances (e.g. from Chile or Kenya), its production may contribute disproportionately to greenhouse gas emissions. At a basic level, consumer choices are rarely clear-cut. Different sustainability issues may be at play and may be in conflict.

At a socio-economic level, moreover, the idea of consumer choice can itself be critiqued from the point of view of environmental sustainability. The consumer society creates needs and desires in order to encourage people to, in simple words, buy more stuff. Increased sales are, of course, good for company profits and generate economic activity that provides jobs and income. But increased sales generally also mean an increase in the use of resources and energy, with a direct impact on the environment through mining, energy production, deforestation and so on. And companies have become adept at 'green' marketing, often offering a green tinge to regular products. A fuel-efficient car, for example, will probably still produce much more emissions per person than public transport.

In this context, what can mathematics teaching really achieve? In some respects, this question presupposes a role for mathematics teaching that we do not directly intend. We are not advocating for mathematics teaching as activism; it is not the role of mathematics teachers to convince their students of the need for any particular action. Given the lack of clarity or certainty about what actions would actually be effective, it is difficult to see how mathematics teachers could unilaterally decide what actions to promote. Instead, we see the role of mathematics teachers as one of preparing students to participate in the debates about environmental sustainability, social justice and economic activity (as linked in the Brundtland Report (United Nations 1987)) that they will encounter during their lives. In other words, we see mathematics teachers as supporting students to learn how to decide for themselves what action to take. It is perhaps worth expanding on this perspective a little more.

Most of the major problems of sustainability facing the world today, several of which we have discussed in this book, are incredibly complex. They involve multiple inter-related problems with environmental, social, political and economic dimensions. Consider one more example: access to fresh water. As the global population increases, many parts of the world are experiencing water supply problems. These problems stem from a mixture of climate change, population growth, changing consumer habits, economic growth, farming, hydro-electricity production and so on. The challenges can include international politics, since rivers cross borders; environmental damage, for example, through the drying up of rivers; and social issues, such as the need to provide clean water for the population. These challenges can lead to tension and potentially even conflict.

Problems like water scarcity, climate change, species loss, or food shortage do not fit the existing approach to problem solving. In the existing approach, priorities are established through political processes, leading to specified policies. For example, the UK government has a policy to reduce greenhouse gas emissions. Scientists are assumed to provide technical information. They evaluate, for example, greenhouse gas emissions, model economic activity and develop projections about the future climate. In this approach to problem-solving, science (including technology and mathematics) is seen as neutral: a source of information and of technical solutions to specified problems. Most members of society do not interact with scientists; and their contribution is, perhaps to a limited extent, understood to be through political processes, such as voting in elections. This kind of approach was reasonably effective in a world that did not think too much about sustainability.

Problems like those discussed in this book cannot, however, be solved in this way. Such problems have a number of features (Funtowicz and Ravetz 1993, 1994). First, they involve contradictions, such as those mentioned above in the context of buying organic food. Similarly, providing fresh water for the population may contradict a desire to preserve habits and protect species diversity. Reducing greenhouse gas emissions contradicts our desire for material comfort. Second, these problems involve uncertainty. Problems involving ecosystems are difficult to describe or measure, as the example about fish stocks illustrates. In the end, we cannot count every creature or even every species of creature; greenhouse gases are difficult to measure; human behaviour, like the weather, is difficult to predict. Third, information cannot be separated from values. Given the uncertainty inherent in such problems, deciding which information to use, which voices to hear and which methods to try depends as much on values as it does on scientific facts. In a debate about water extraction, for example, should more weight be given to the people whose lives will be affected by the removal of water, or those who will benefit from the increase in supply? (This is a real and current problem: the city of Las Vegas in the USA recently proposed to extract huge amounts of water from sparsely populated river valleys 300 miles from the city (Goldenburg, 2012)). Given these features, the relationship between science and the wider public needs to change from one of subservience to one of dialogue (Funtowicz and Ravetz 1993, 1994).

In the context of this kind of complex problem-solving, it is, we argue, no longer sufficient to teach students mathematics as a separate body of facts and methods that rarely reaches beyond the classroom, apart from the occasional 'real world' word problem. To engage in sustainability problems means that future citizens need to be able to engage in dialogue with scientists and policy-makers. They need, in other words, to participate in the transformation of their society. And they cannot do so effectively without mathematics; mathematics, moreover, not just as facts and methods, but as something that formats our lives as part of the structure of society (Barwell 2013). Teaching mathematics as if the planet matters is not, then, about changing students' minds, but about preparing them to participate in solving the sustainability problems they will face in their lives.

References

Barwell, R. (2013) The mathematical formatting of climate change: critical mathematics education and post-normal science. *Research in Mathematics Education* 15(1), 1–16.

Funtowicz, S. O. and Ravetz, J. R. (1993) Science for the post-normal age. *Futures* 25(7) 739–55.

Funtowicz, S. O. and Ravetz, J. R. (1994) Emergent complex systems. *Futures* 26(6) 568–82.

Goldenburg, S. (2012) Las Vegas plans to pump water across 300 miles of desert approved. *The Guardian*. Available online at http://www.guardian.co.uk/environment/2012/mar/23/las-vegas-pump-water-approved?intcmp=239 (accessed 01 December 2012).

Skovsmose, O. (1984) Mathematical education and democracy, *Educational Studies in Mathematics*, 21: 109–28.

United Nations (1987) *Our common future: World Commission on Environment and Development*. Oxford: Oxford University Press.

Index

Bold page numbers indicate figures, *italic* numbers indicate tables.

Teacher and child: a book for parents (Ginott) 82–3

teaching mathematics: climate change 40; critical mathematics education 10–12, 34–5; day-to-day/average temperatures 43–4; emissions data 47; identity, teachers' 91–3; knowing, three forms of 12–14; knowledge, forms of drawn on 91–2; reflection and critique in 93–6; role models for 92; and sustainability 8–10, 165–6; temperature, norms and anomalies in 40; thematic approach 94–6; Trading Game 24–7; *see also* critical mathematics education

technological knowing 12–13, 34, 51, 54

technology: climate change 34; mathematics as embedded in 11–12, 34, 163

teenage births *78*

temperature: day-to-day, impact of climate change on 41–4, **42,** *43, 44;* norms and anomalies in 36–40, *37, 38,* **39, 40**

Towards a Philosophy of Critical Mathematics Education (Skovsmose) 94

Trading Game 24–7

transformation: approach to sustainability 8, 9, *9;* integrated curriculum 164; mathematics 77

unemployment/employment 80–1, *81*

Universal Declaration of Human Rights 74–5

van Hiele, P. 134

waste and recycling activity 124–9, **125**

Watson, Reg 61

weather distinguished from climate 32

Wilkinson, Richard 75–80, *78*